The Good Night, Sleep Tight WORKBOOK

NEWBORN TO FIVE YEARS

Gentle Proven Solutions to Help Your Child Sleep Well and Wake Up Happy

The Sleep Lady®
KIM WEST, LCSW-C

Edited by Maura Rhodes,
former Senior Editor, *Parenting* Magazine

ESP
easton studio
press

Published by

Easton Studio Press

P.O. Box 3131

Westport, CT 06880

(203) 571-0781

www.eastonsp.com

Visit Kim West, The Sleeplady at www.sleeplady.com

Book and cover design by Barbara Aronica-Buck

Print ISBN: 978-0979824-86-9

eBook ISBN: 978-1-935212-18-8

Manufactured in the USA

Fifth printing, February 2017

10 9 8 7 6 5

D0028726

Contents

Introduction

 I'm Kim West, a licensed child and family therapist and the mother of two girls. My clients know me as The Sleep Lady®. For over ten years, I've focused my practice on helping tens of thousands of weary, bleary-eyed parents all over the world find solutions to their children's sleep problems—from babies who are old enough to sleep through the night but aren't yet doing so, to nap-resistant toddlers, to older kids who won't stay in their beds (or sneak into their parents' beds uninvited). My method, the Sleep Lady® Shuffle, depends on step-by-step changes in the bedtime, nap time, and middle-of-the-night routines that haven't been working for these families. For the parents of infants in particular, it's a gentler alternative to letting their babies "cry it out." Ultimately, the children I work with develop sleep "independence" and can drift off on their own and sleep soundly throughout the night, knowing that Mom and Dad are nearby.

What makes the Sleep Lady® method so successful is that it's not a "one size fits all" approach to sleep coaching. When I work with a family individually, I factor in their values, lifestyle, and childrearing philosophies so as not to suggest something that might make parents feel uncomfortable. Doing so would be highly counterproductive—I can't stress this enough—and so a plan that parents can't stick with is bound to fail.

That said, the Sleep Lady® Shuffle is not an overnight cure.

Essentially, you're teaching your child a new skill. So be patient and remember that mastering a skill—whether it's walking, handling a spoon, using the potty, or sleeping through the night—takes time. However, the families I work with solve the majority of their kids' bedtime snafus within two weeks. (Issues like napping and early rising typically take a little longer.)

How to Use This Workbook

For the best results, I recommend that you read the first few chapters, plus the chapter that corresponds to your child's age, of my book *Good Night, Sleep Tight* before you begin creating your plan (on page 46 of this workbook); at the very least, please read all the way through the workbook before you start sleep coaching your child. And remember: Your success will depend on consistency, follow-through, and patience, as well as 100 percent commitment on the part of everyone else who shares in caring for your child—including your partner, your child's grandparents, and the sitter.

May you enjoy many peaceful nights of sleep ahead!

— Kim West, LCSW-C
The Sleep Lady®

Disclaimer: The information and advice presented in this book have been reviewed by a qualified pediatrician. It should not, however, substitute for the advice of your family doctor or other trained health care professionals. You are advised to consult with a health care professional with regard to all matters that may require medical attention or diagnosis for your baby or child, and you should check with a physician before administering or undertaking any course of treatment such as sleep training your baby or child.

The Good Night, Sleep Tight
WORKBOOK

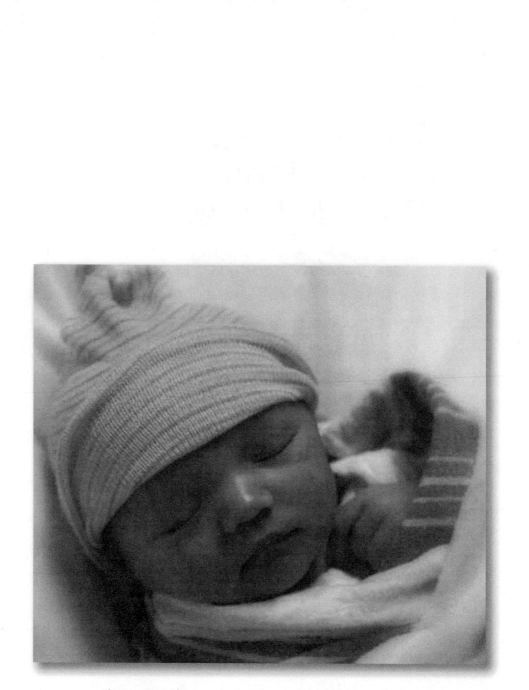

Liam, age 1 day

CHAPTER ONE

Before You Begin
Sleep Coaching

I firmly believe that a solid understanding of important sleep principles is key for a sleep-training plan to work. I realize you may be eager to get started and tempted to skip this chapter, but if you haven't read *Good Night, Sleep Tight*, then this chapter (and the next) are *critical to your success*.

Even if you've read *Good Night, Sleep Tight*, skip down and review the chapters on **consistency** and **avoiding intermittent reinforcement** on pages 6–7. Given that we all need to hear things at least three times before we can *really* understand them, and the fact that you're probably too tired to remember much these days anyway, it's vital that you take the time to refresh your memory about these important concepts.

Need-to-Know Sleep Facts

- **Regular sleep time is key.** Going to bed at the same time each night and getting up at the same time each morning is vital for children. The consistency keeps their internal body clock, a.k.a. circadian rhythm, on track, which in turn ensures that they get quality sleep. Even adults should have regular bed- and wake-up times; **it's okay if we vary our own routine on weekends, but only by one hour.**

If you miss your child's natural time to sleep—in other words, her "sleep window"—her body will begin to secrete hormones, including one called cortisol, which acts like a mild form of adrenaline and can leave her too wired to get to sleep easily. (I imagine this must feel much like trying to nod off when you're tired but have had too much caffeine.) Eventually, after you've both endured a good deal of crying, your child *will* fall asleep. "Thank goodness," you'll think, "at least she'll sleep late tomorrow." Logical, but incorrect. Having missed her regular bedtime, she'll actually sleep *less* soundly and she'll wake earlier than usual. This can then lead to poor naps the next day, a disrupted bedtime that night—and the beginning of a vicious cycle that will be tough to break.

- **Quality of sleep is just as important as quantity.** Besides the right amount of sleep (for age-by-age sleep requirements, see Chapter 2), a child needs:

  the right *kind* of sleep—unfragmented, uninterrupted (except in the case of newborns who still need to nurse or take a bottle during the night), and motionless: the movement of, say, a baby swing prevents the brain from going into a deep sleep and is not as restorative.

  to sleep at the right times—in other words, his bedtime, wake-up time, and naps are all in sync with his natural sleep patterns.

  sleep that's undisturbed by medical problems such as asthma, allergies, reflux, or obstructive sleep apnea or other physical sleep disorders.

- **Babies must be *taught* to put themselves to sleep: It's a learned skill.** Putting your baby in her crib when she's "drowsy but awake," will give her the opportunity to get herself to sleep on her own. If you have trouble visualizing what "drowsy but awake" means, imagine a scale of one to ten, one being wide awake and ten being deeply asleep. You want to put your baby down at around a seven or eight on the drowsy scale. She should be warm, fed, comforted, and clearly sleepy, but alert enough to know that she's going into the crib.

When you put your baby down at the right point on the drowsiness scale, she'll probably protest. This is normal; no need to get her out and restart her bedtime routine. Instead, stay nearby and use physical and verbal reassurance to comfort her, and soon she'll learn to transition from drowsiness to sleep without fussing. I will go over this in more detail in Chapter 3.

Note that you don't want your baby to fall asleep too quickly: If she conks out in less than five minutes, she was probably already so far gone when you put her down that she wasn't aware of being transferred from your arms to her crib. And without that lack of awareness, she won't learn her sleep "lesson." Get her into bed when she's a tad less drowsy the next time.

Incidentally, "drowsy but awake" becomes less important as children get older. With toddlers and preschoolers, a calming bedtime routine of reading and songs prepares them for slumber. Of course, make sure you're not falling asleep with them during those soothing bedtime stories!

- **A child's ability to put himself to sleep is important not just at bedtime, but also when he wakes in the night or during a nap.** Just as adults do, children have cycles of non-REM (deep) sleep and REM (light) sleep. A child's sleep cycles do not mimic a grown-up's until around the age of 2. When a sleeper of any age moves from one cycle to the next, his brain experiences a "partial arousal," in which he'll wake up just enough to roll over, realize he's thirsty, or notice a fallen pillow; then, if he doesn't need to get up for that glass of water or to retrieve that pillow, he'll go right back to sleep. For babies who sleep through the night, partial arousals take place approximately every three to four hours (during naps, they occur after 10 minutes and 30 minutes of sleep); this means that during a partial arousal they may open their eyes and even realize that they're alone in the crib—and think, "Oh, I'm in my room, there's my lovey . . ." and put themselves back to sleep.

- **It's vital for a baby to learn to put herself to sleep without a "sleep crutch"—in other words, a negative sleep association that requires something be done either to or for her in order for her to go to sleep.** Some examples of common sleep crutches are nursing, bottle-feeding, rocking, walking, and having a parent lie down with a baby or young child until she falls asleep. These activities are labeled "negative" because a child can't do them for herself.

> **SLEEP-TIGHT TIP**
>
> Putting oneself to sleep is a *learned* skill. Gently guiding our children to master this skill is just as important as teaching them their ABCs.

- **"Positive sleep associations,"** on the other hand, are self-soothing behaviors or rituals that a baby can create for herself, such as sucking her thumb or fingers, twirling her hair, stroking a stuffed animal or favorite blanket, rubbing things against her cheek, rocking her body, humming, or singing.

- **Phasing out a sleep crutch can be as challenging for the parent as the baby.** After all, you've come to rely on the magic of rocking, nursing, swinging, or pacing your baby all the way to the Land of Nod too. It can be really hard to give that up, but ultimately you want to get to the point where you can stop *before* your baby drifts off completely. Try cutting the amount of time you walk or rock your little one before putting him in his crib. Note that some babies get upset when "teased" with enough walking or rocking to make them drowsy but not enough to put them to sleep—in which case a more drastic approach is necessary: a minute of walking or rocking—just long enough to say, "I love you," say a prayer, or hum a short lullaby—before being put down. If you have to choose between too drowsy or too awake, choose awake, and then work on soothing your baby to a drowsier point in the crib.

If you nurse or bottle-feed your baby to sleep, you can try making feeding an earlier part of the bedtime routine. Or, leave a dim light on so you can see when she's starting to drift off (and to lessen the association in her mind between eating and falling asleep). Watch her closely: When she stops sucking energetically and swallowing (and instead is suckling gently, with a sort of fluttering motion), she's past the "drowsy" target. At this point, you have two choices:

Unlatch her from your breast or the bottle, put her in her crib, and try to catch her a little earlier at the next bedtime. If she wakes up while you're unlatching her and gives you a look that says, "Hey, I'm still hungry! I didn't mean to fall asleep on the job!" then give her one more chance. If she wakes up enough to really eat, let her finish. But if she goes back to that fluttery business, you've been duped! She's not hungry—she just wants to suckle herself to sleep. Unlatch her, burp her, give her a kiss, and put her to bed.

- or -

Arouse her by changing her diaper or loosening her pajamas. Say your soothing good-night words, and place her in her crib awake.

- **Children need morning rituals just as much as they need bedtime rituals to help reinforce their understanding of wake-up time versus sleep time.** When it's time to start the day, do a "dramatic wake-up." Open the blinds, switch on the lights, sing some cheery good-morning songs, and welcome the new day.

As you read further into this workbook, you'll see how I use dramatic wake-up to help your child differentiate between when you're going to get them out of their crib or bed. Let's say your child wakes at 5:00 a.m. and you go to her and sit next to her crib or bed to help her back to sleep. At 6:00 a.m. she's still wide awake with no sign of going back to sleep, and you wish to give up on the night (6:00 a.m. is the earliest I ever want you to give up on the night). I would not want you to stand and pick her up and start the day fearing that you might train her to cry on and off for one hour (see intermitten reinforcement below). Instead I want you to leave the room, count to 10, go back in, turn on the light and say, "Good morning!" and start your day.

An Important Note on Consistency: Once you have a sleep-training plan in place, it's *absolutely crucial to be consistent*—even in the middle of the night when you're tired and not thinking clearly. Sending mixed messages—which behavioral scientists call "intermittent reinforcement"— to your child throughout the day (and night!) will only frustrate him. He won't be able to decipher what type of behavior merits rewards and what type of behavior doesn't. Inconsistently reinforced behavior is the hardest type of behavior to modify or extinguish. It takes longer to change and it always gets worse before it gets better. This is particularly true of a child who's more than 1 year old.

Here are three examples of intermittent reinforcement with children and sleep that I want you to *avoid*:

1. "Sometimes I feed you to sleep and sometimes I don't." For example, you may nurse your baby to sleep, feed him if he wakes after 10:00 p.m., rock him to sleep if he wakes again before 1:00 a.m., and then finally bring him into your bed out of desperation. This causes confusion. I want you to work toward putting your child down to bed drowsy but awake and responding to him consistently the same way through out the night.

2. "Sometimes I've let you cry for 15 or 30 minutes because I was desperate and heard this approach might work—but then I couldn't take it anymore and went in, picked you up, and rocked you to sleep." This is an example of how you can train your child to cry until you put him to sleep—any way you can!

3. "Sometimes I bring you in to my bed—but only after 5:00 a.m." Please remember that your child can't tell time. Why wouldn't he expect to come to your bed at 2:00 a.m. if you bring him in after 5:00?

Keep in mind too, that children actually *crave* consistency at bedtime (and all the time, for that matter). When they know what to expect, and what's expected of them, it reassures them and helps them feel safe and sound.

> **SLEEP-TIGHT TIP**
>
> Consistency is truly the key to parenting and especially sleep training success.

How to Prep for Sleep Coaching Success: Steps to Take before You Start

1. Get the green light from your child's doctor.

Most sleep problems are behavioral, but you should still have your pediatrician rule out any underlying medical conditions that may be contributing to your child's sleep issues, such as reflux, asthma, allergies, ear infections, or sleep apnea. Make sure medications, including over-the-counter remedies, aren't disturbing her sleep.

If you're still feeding your baby during the night, ask her doctor if, given your child's age, weight, and general health, she still *needs* wee-hour nourishment. Review with your pediatrician how much your child is eating during her waking hours.

2. Keep a sleep-and-feeding log.

Chances are, your short-term memory isn't quite up to par as a result of sleep deprivation: Your days and nights are going by in a blur.

But in order to figure out how to solve your child's sleep problem, you'll need to have a clear picture of what's happening at bedtime and during the night, what's working, what's not, how your baby is responding, etc. Keep track by writing it all down for a few days or a week. Having a record in writing, instead of relying on scrambled mental notes in your sleep-deprived brain, will give you a more accurate picture of your child's patterns and your own responses.

Some parents find it easiest to keep a log for scribbling on right next to their child's bed. Look for signs of his natural bedtime window. Jot down when and how often he wakes up during the night. Note what you did to get him back to sleep, whether you rocked him, nursed him, sang to him, or brought him into your bed. Compare your child's daily schedule with the typical schedules I suggest in Chapter 2.

Once you start my program, continue your log. Tracking your child's sleep patterns will help you figure out what's working, what's not, and what tactics you should tweak. At the end of this workbook is a sample log you can use. (Feel free to come up with your own format if you don't like mine.)

3. Figure out your child's ideal bedtime.

This is the period of time during which she'll show signs that she's ready to sleep—yawning, rubbing her eyes, twisting her hair, fussing. Often parents miss a child's sleepy cues—especially in the evening, because it's such a busy time of day. They may be cleaning up the dinner dishes, shuffling through the mail, helping an older child with homework, etc. Pay extra attention to how your child behaves between 6:00 p.m. and 8:00 p.m. (and make sure she's not zoning out in front of the television). As soon as she begins acting drowsy, you'll know that that's her natural bedtime—and the time at which you should be putting her down each evening going forward.

Although I usually recommend making bedtime adjustments gradually, 30 minutes or so at a time, sometimes with a child under 3 you can make the changes quickly if you learn to recognize her natural patterns. For instance, if your 20-month-old is used to going to bed at 10:00 p.m., but you can see that she's drowsy at 7:30 p.m., you don't need to spend days gradually adjusting. Just put her to bed at 7:30 p.m. and make sure you do so again the next night and the night after that.

If you have trouble picking up on your child's drowsy signals, you can pinpoint a reasonable bedtime for her simply by looking at when she normally wakes up and factoring in how much sleep she should be getting based on her age. (You'll find sleep averages on pages 15–26.) Let's say you have a 2-year-old who tends to wake up by 7:00 a.m. every morning. The average 2-year-old needs 11 hours of sleep at night, so that would mean that your child needs to have gone through her entire bedtime routine and be *sound asleep* by 8:00 p.m.

4. Create a relaxing bedtime routine.

All children, from newborns on up to school-age kids, need a set of comforting and predictable rituals to help them prepare physically and psychologically for sleep. These activities should be calm, quiet ones, like reading, story-telling, or lullabies; bedtime is not the time for tickling, wrestling, scary stories, or TV shows, or anything else that's stimulating. Because you're preparing your little one to be separated from you for the night, the tone should be serene and reassuring. For babies over 6 months old, I encourage attachment to a "lovey," a favorite stuffed animal or blanket that he can use to comfort himself when he wakes during the night. And with the exception of baths and tooth-brushing, the bedtime routine should take place in the child's nursery or bedroom

SLEEP-TIGHT TIP

If your child hates some aspect of bedtime, get that part over with first. For instance, if she can't stand having her teeth brushed, do it right after her bath, not after you've read two books and gotten her all snug and cozy.

Here are some activities that work well as part of a bedtime routine, depending on a child's age. Three from this list is plenty:

- bath
- put on pajamas
- brush teeth
- go potty
- massage
- swaddle
- read books
- sing a short song
- play a quiet game
- share three things about your day
- tell a story
- listen to music
- baby or toddler yoga
- small sippy cup of water with books
- bottle or nursing
- prayers, blessings, or sending kisses and love to others
- plenty of hugs and kisses

- **Install room-darkening shades** if your child's bedroom gets too much light, he wakes up very early, or has trouble napping; but leave a dim night-light on so that you can see him when you check on him. He'll probably sleep more soundly with that little bit of light too, although some children do better in total darkness.

- **Consider playing white noise or nature music** if your child's room isn't very soundproof and you have a barking dog, loud neighbors, older siblings, live on a busy street, etc. Children do learn to sleep through routine household sounds (and they should to a large extent), but some places are just really loud and some kids are really sensitive. White noise is a constant sound that helps to block out noise; you can buy a white noise machine, or try turning on a fan. I discourage using music to mask noise; kids can get too dependent on it—meaning they'll want someone to come in and restart their music every time they wake up.

7. Decide about the pacifier.

Research shows that pacifier use during sleep time may reduce the risk of sudden infant death syndrome, or SIDS, among babies who are 6 months or younger. Medical advice on pacifiers has changed frequently over the years, and it may well change again. Please check with your doctor, and check in again as your baby gets a little older. If you're breast-feeding, wait four to six weeks until nursing is well established before you introduce the pacifier. Bottle-fed babies can start earlier.

Even if you use the pacifier when the baby sleeps, you may choose not to use it all the time when she's awake and fussy. You can reconsider how and when you want her to continue with the pacifier when she gets to be about 6 months old.

If your baby is over 6 months old and is using a pacifier, you may need to decide if it is a problem that needs addressing during sleep coaching.

Ask yourself the following:

- Can she grip and maneuver it into her mouth on her own (most babies can do this by 8 months old)?

- Are you making multiple trips to her crib to replug the pacifier?

- Have you spoken to your pediatrician about weaning your child off the pacifier?

Your choices:

- If you find yourself having to repeatedly replug your child's pacifier and your pediatrician has signed off on getting rid of it, then you will have to pick the big night. Unfortunately you can't really "wean" a child from the pacifier. It's either in the baby's mouth or it isn't. Pick the first night you will put your child to bed without it. You'll have to do some extra soothing for the first few nights. I give more details on stopping the pacifier in the age chapters of *Good Night, Sleep Tight*. Some children give it up by themselves.

8. Get your child used to waking up between 6:00 a.m. and 7:30 a.m.

This applies to babies over 5 months of age who are waking up at all different times, sometimes as late as 8:30 or 9:30 a.m., which then throws off the entire day and confuses their internal clocks. Start waking your baby by 7:30 a.m. about five days before you plan to start sleep coaching.

9. Make sure all of your child's caregivers are on board.

It's vital that your spouse, partner, nanny, and anyone else who frequently cares for your child understands each aspect of the sleep-training plan (and why it's important) and is willing to follow through. This is key to maintaining the consistency that's so vital to sleep success. (See Nap Coaching on page 37 for what to do when you have a reluctant babysitter, and also how to work around your baby's schedule if he's in day care.)

10. Pick a realistic start date.

Choose a block of time, ideally about three weeks, during which you don't expect any major disruptions or changes in your household, including trips, moving, or the arrival of a new baby. Some families decide to start sleep coaching during a summer or winter vacation so the grown-ups won't have to juggle sleep training with work. That's a good strategy, but be careful to keep your child's schedule consistent even if yours is not. For instance, don't introduce a nice, sensible 7:30 p.m. bedtime the very week you plan to let her stay up until 10:00 with the grandparents on Christmas Eve, or are going to have a horde of entertaining young cousins camping out in your backyard over the Fourth of July.

CHAPTER TWO

Age-Specific Sleep Averages and Typical Day Schedules

 Most parents ask me what a "typical day" of feedings, naps, and bedtime would look like for their child, so what follows are *typical* schedules for kids at specific ages and stages. Please note that they apply to generally healthy children with no growth or developmental concerns, and are based on recommendations from the American Academy of Pediatrics. However, they're *very flexible, so you don't need to adhere to them too rigidly.* Your own child's routine should be based on careful observation of his eating and sleep cues, and also on input from your pediatrician.

Newborns: Getting Off to a Good Sleep Start

I don't recommend formal sleep training for infants until after 4 months. However, you can *gently shape* a newborn's sleep habits early on, and hopefully help to prevent future sleep problems, with the *Sleep Lady's® Rules for Infant Slumber* (you can read about them in more detail in *Good Night, Sleep Tight*).

1. Create a flexible feeding and sleeping routine. Not a minute-by-minute schedule but a sensible framework. The predictability is calming for a baby, and will help you get better at reading your baby's signals and clues.

2. Use a variety of soothing techniques to see what works for your baby.

Benjamin, age 6 months

3. Offer a pacifier for soothing and sucking but don't let it become a sleep crutch.

4. Sometimes feed your baby when he wakes up after a nap—not just when you are trying to get him to sleep.

5. Put him down drowsy but awake at least once every 24 hours.

6. If you are returning to work outside of the home, introduce one bottle a day—even if you are committed to breast feeding, as I was with my own children—around the third or fourth week if breastfeeding has been established.

7. Create a sleep-friendly environment.

8. Carefully think through the question of bedsharing (or co-sleeping) and roomsharing. Know how to co-sleep safely if that's your choice. But if you don't want to co-sleep, don't get into the habit simply because you don't know how to avoid it.

The First Month (0 to 4 weeks)

Total sleep is 16 to 18 hours, half during the night and half spread out over four daytime naps. By the end of the first month, babies sleep an average of 15½ to 17 hours total—about 8½ to 10 hours at night and 6 to 7 hours during the day spread over three or four naps. They wake up two to three times at night for feedings but should go back to sleep quickly.

According to the American Academy of Pediatrics, once the mother's milk comes in, newborns may feed as often as every 1½ hours, and they shouldn't go more than three hours without eating, for a total of eight to 12 feedings in 24 hours. Formula-fed babies will eat less frequently, two to three ounces every three or four hours, for a total of six to eight feedings a day.

YOUR TASK THIS MONTH is to help your baby differentiate day sleep from night sleep by:

- not allowing her to get overstimulated (keep her out of brightly lit, overly loud environments).

- preventing her from becoming overtired (she should only be awake for 1½ to 2 hours at a time during the day).

- exposing her to natural light or turning on the lights when she's awake during the day.

- waking her after three hours of daytime sleep to feed her (you want to save those long stretches of slumber for night time).

The Second Month (5 to 8 weeks)

Total sleep is 15½ to 17 hours: 8½ to 10 hours at night and 6 to 7 hours during the day spread over three to four naps. By the end of this month some babies will wake only once a night to be fed; some will still need two middle-of-the night feedings. Nighttime sleep becomes more organized (meaning your baby will begin to sleep longer and more deeply at night) and by 6 to 8 weeks you may see a 4- or even 5-hour stretch at night.

Breastfed babies will still need to eat about every 2 to 2½ hours, although some will go 3 hours. The normal range is anything from 8 to 12 feedings in 24 hours. Formula-fed babies will probably take about four ounces per feeding, about every 3 to 4 hours.

Your task this month is to establish a consistent bedtime routine:

- At 6 weeks, start putting your baby down "drowsy but awake" at bedtime.

- Between 6 and 8 weeks, focus on helping him to fall asleep *without* a breast or bottle in his mouth, or by being rocked until he's totally out. Sit by his side and pat him, *sh-sh-sh* him, or pick him up if need be to calm him, but then put him back down. Stay by his side until he dozes off.

Don't worry about scheduled naps yet; your baby's daytime sleep won't be organized at this age, and he'll still nap while you're on the run. Enjoy this flexibility while you can! Late-afternoon and early evening fussiness begins now and usually ends around 12 weeks.

The Third Month (9 to 12 weeks)

Total sleep is 15 hours: 10 hours at night and 5 hours spread out over three to four daytime naps. Many babies toward the end of this month can sleep 6 to 8 hours at a stretch during the night.

Breastfed babies still need to eat every three hours or so, but they don't need to eat as frequently at night. Bottle-fed babies will typically take 4 to 5 ounces every three to four hours.

YOUR TASKS THIS MONTH

- Continue to put your baby down drowsy but awake at bedtime.

- Move her from her bassinette or co-sleeper bed to her own crib (unless you're planning to practice the family bed for the long term).

- Your baby's bedtime should be around 10:00 or 11:00 p.m. at the beginning of this period; start moving it earlier (to about 8:00 p.m.) once she can sleep for eight hours at a time and/or when you notice that she's getting tired earlier.

- Her daytime nap schedule won't fall into place until the end of this month. Meanwhile, don't let her get overtired: Use the swing, stroller or baby sling to make sure she naps during the afternoon.

The Fourth and Fifth Months

Total sleep is 10 to 11 hours at night and 4 to 5 hours spread out over three naps during the day. At 4 months babies should be able to sleep about 8 hours at night without a feeding, and by 5 months they go for about 10 or 11 hours.

A breastfed baby will need to eat at least five times a day, every three to four hours (but don't be surprised if during a growth spurt he wants to nurse every two to three hours!).

By five months, you may be able to stretch the interval between meals closer to four hours. A formula-fed baby will eat less frequently, adding about an ounce per feeding each month, so that by the end of the fifth month he'll be taking 6 to 8 ounces at a time, at four or five feedings in 24 hours. (In general, a bottle-fed baby shouldn't take more than 32 ounces of formula during a 24-hour period.)

YOUR TASKS THIS MONTH

- Get your baby to bed between 8:00 p.m. and 9:00 p.m. If he consistently falls asleep during his before-bed feeding, move his bedtime earlier.

- Start reducing middle-of-the-night feedings. You can do this by either feeding him just once during the night—the first time he wakes up (as long as he's been asleep for at least two hours) or by offering him a "dream feed" just before you turn in yourself—in other words, getting him up around 10:00 or 11:00 p.m. See *Good Night, Sleep Tight* for more details.

- If he's able to put himself to sleep independently at bedtime and is getting up once at night for a quick businesslike meal and then going right back to sleep, I would leave it alone. He'll probably outgrow that last feeding soon. If not, you'll learn how to gently end it at 6 or 7 months in Chapter 5.

- Don't nurse your baby or give him a bottle right before each nap. Feeding him when he's up and alert, instead of ready to go to bed, helps weaken the food-sleep association and reinforces the message that he can get to sleep and stay asleep without a breast or bottle.

- Help lengthen, organize, and improve his naps:

  - Watch both the clock and his behavior to know when its time to put him down for a nap.

  - Nap him in his crib for all naps except the last nap.

  - Naps should be longer then 45 minutes and ideally 90 minutes or longer. If your baby is cat napping, go to him when he wakes up and help comfort him back to sleep.

Experiment to see what soothing technique works the best. Be patient and try to resettle him for 20–30 minutes. He may reward you with another 45 minutes of sleep! Slowly phase out your intervention as he gets better at learning to put himself back to sleep.

Typical Feeding and Sleep Routines

Note that these are numbers are averages: Some children need more or less sleep than others, (although variations should not be huge), and not all kids are ready for a nap at the exact same time each day. It's more important to watch for your child's sleep cues— eye-rubbing, a lull in activity, fussing, noises she makes that are unique to your child—than it is to watch the clock, so that you can get her to sleep before she gets overtired.

6 TO 8 MONTHS

Average sleep: 10 to 12 hours at night (without needing to eat), 3½ hours during the day (two to three naps). Some babies this age may need one feeding during the night. Your pediatrician can help you figure out what's best for your child. Many children this age take a small third nap in the afternoon, depending on how long their second nap lasted.

(Shift earlier if your child wakes between 6:00 a.m. and 7:00 a.m.)

7:00 a.m.–7:30 a.m.	Wake up; diaper change; breakfast (nurse or bottle feed plus solids).
9:00 a.m.–9:30 a.m.	Start the morning nap, 45 minutes minimum to 1½ hours maximum. When baby wakes up, nurse/bottle feed plus solids.
12:30 p.m.–1:30 p.m.	Start the afternoon nap. Baby should be asleep within 2 to 3 hours of waking from his morning nap and sleep for 1½ to 2 hours. Upon awakening, nurse/bottle feed.

3:30 a.m.–4:00 p.m.	Optional short third nap depends on previous nap time, about 45 minutes to 1 hour.

Window from afternoon nap to bedtime should not exceed 4 hours.

5:00 p.m.–5:30 p.m.	Nurse/bottle feed plus solids.
6:00 p.m.–6:30 p.m.	Start bath/bedtime preparations, which may include giving a bottle or nursing.
7:00 p.m.–7:30 p.m.	Bedtime.

9 TO 12 MONTHS

Average sleep for a 9-month-old: 11 hours at night, 3 hours during the day (two naps). Most 9-month-olds on a solid two-nap-a-day schedule are ready to or already have given up their small third nap.

Average sleep for a 12-month-old: 11¼ hours at night, 2½ hours during the day (two naps).

(Shift earlier if your child wakes between 6:00 a.m. and 7:00 a.m.)

7:00 a.m.–7:30 a.m.	Wake up. Nurse/bottle/cup and breakfast.
9:00 a.m.–9:30 a.m.	Start the morning nap. If your child is sleeping 11 to 12 hours uninterrupted at night he might be able to stay awake until 10:00 a.m. (or 3 hours after waking up). Some children need a small morning snack after the nap.
12:00 p.m.–12:30 p.m.	Lunch with nurse/bottle or cup.
1:00 p.m.–2:00 p.m.	Start the afternoon nap. Snack upon awakening.
5:00 p.m.–6:00 p.m.	Dinner with nurse/bottle or cup.

Changes and Challenges: Weaning and Transitioning to a Cup

- Some babies are ready to give up the breast or bottle during this time (or Mom and Dad are ready for them to!). If a child isn't generally overtired or doesn't need a feeding to get to sleep, weaning should be an easy, natural transition. Some signs a baby may be ready to move on from the breast or bottle:

  1. She looks around while nursing or feeding

  2. She mouths the nipple without sucking

  3. She tries to slide off your lap before polishing off a bottle or emptying your breast

- It's a good idea to introduce your baby to a cup by 9 months old, so by the time she's 12 months old (or very soon after), she'll be taking *all* liquids from one. Do your best to stick to this guideline: Around 15 months, many babies become attached to objects like bottles and pacifiers, so if your child is still drinking from a bottle at this age (especially before going to sleep), it's going to be especially tough to wean her off of it.

12 TO 18 MONTHS
Average sleep: 11¼ hours straight at night, 2¼ to 2½ hours during the day (two naps for a 12-month-old; one nap for an 18-month-old)

Typical meals: three meals and two snacks

(Shift earlier if your child wakes between 6:00 and 7:00 a.m.)

7:00 a.m.–7:30 a.m.	Wake-up and breakfast.
9:00 a.m.–9:30 a.m.	Start of one-hour morning nap if she's still taking one.

11:30 a.m.–12:30 p.m.	Lunch (depending on morning nap timing).
12:30–1:30 p.m.	Start of afternoon nap. About 1½ hours if it's a second nap, between 2 and 2½ hours if it's the only nap of the day.
5:00 p.m.–5:30 p.m.	Dinner.
6:00 p.m.–6:30 p.m.	Start bath/bedtime routine.
7:00 p.m.––8:00 p.m.	Asleep.

Some toddlers need a longer transition from dinner to bedtime, and should eat earlier than the rest of the family. However, most children this age don't *need* a meal before bedtime, although some like to nurse briefly (if they're still breastfeeding) for comfort. This is okay, as long as they aren't nursing to sleep.

Changes and Challenges: Dropping the Morning Nap

Most toddlers are ready to give up their morning nap between 15 and 18 months, and nearly all children go through the "one nap is too little, two naps are too many" phase. All you can do is make the transition as smooth as possible, although even in the best-case scenario, a child may be cranky and out-of-sorts for two or three weeks. Your toddler has reached this milestone when she:

- *consistently* gets 10 to 11 hours of uninterrupted sleep at night. If she's not, work on improving nighttime sleep before you tackle the nap change.

- *consistently* takes longer and longer to fall asleep for her morning nap.

- *consistently* takes increasingly shorter morning naps *or* sleeps for too long in the morning and then refuses an afternoon nap.

Once you see these changes in your child's sleep and nap behavior for at least 10 to 14 days straight, you can start the process of dropping her morning nap. It should take only 7 to 10 days. Here's how:

SLEEP-TIGHT TIP

 Between 12 and 14 months your child will begin actively dreaming. This can startle her awake. It's fine to go to her to reassure her; just don't revert to your sleep crutch to get her back to sleep.

1. Gradually push her morning nap later—until around 11:00 a.m. for two days, then 11:30 for a couple of days, then noon, and so on. Don't let the nap get stuck in late morning. Some kids can adapt more quickly to a noon nap time and others need to go slower. Watch your child. Your goal is for the afternoon nap to start between 12:30 and 1:00 and last at least 2¼ to 2½ hours.

2. If your toddler sleeps for only an hour and wakes up tired, then try to soothe and resettle her back to sleep. If all else fails, use one of your emergency techniques, like putting her in the car or stroller.

3. Do not let her sleep past 4:00 or 4:30 p.m., so as not to disrupt her bedtime.

4. Try to get your child to bed earlier than usual for two weeks or so during the transition—like 7:00 p.m.—to cushion her from being overtired.

5. Be open to an occasional "two-nap day." If during the transition your child seems too tired, it's okay to let her nap twice—just limit the morning snooze to 45 minutes.

6. If your child is in childcare or preschool part of the time, try to synchronize the afternoon nap at home with the timetable at school (assuming she starts her nap at school between 12:00 and 1:00 p.m.).

18 MONTHS TO 2½ YEARS

Average sleep for an 18-month-old: 11¼ hours at night, 2¼ hours during the day (one nap).

Average sleep for a 2-year-old: 11 hours at night, 2 hours during the day (one nap).

7:00 a.m.–7:30 a.m.	Wake-up and breakfast.
12 p.m.–12:30 p.m.	Lunch.
12:30 p.m. – 1:00 p.m.	Start afternoon nap.
5:00 p.m.–5:30 p.m.	Dinner.
6:00 p.m.–6:30 p.m.	Start bath/bedtime routine.
7:00 p.m.–8:00 p.m.	Bedtime.

A soothing bedtime routine is a must for older toddlers. Most kids this age will demand that you do everything in the same order each night, and not leave anything out, so limit the bedtime regimen to a manageable number of elements (*one* story plus *one* song plus *one* cuddle in the rocking chair). Starting around age 2, you may see a lot of stalling and delay tactics. If your child "needs" frequent tucking in, another kiss, etc., respond *once*. The second time he calls for you, be neutral but firm and say, "No more tuck-ins. Now it's time to go to sleep," and stand your ground: If you say, "Last time" and then give in, you're sending the message that if your tyke begs and cries long enough, he'll get what he wants. If you and your partner take turns putting your child to bed, it's perfectly fine if your styles are slightly different. Just make sure that you're consistent about when bedtime takes place and how you respond to delay tactics.

Changes and Challenges: Climbing out of the Crib

Many toddlers in this age group try climbing out of the crib. I almost always advise parents to keep him in as long as possible, definitely until 2½ years old and preferably until 3. By then, a child has the verbal skills to understand the "big bed" rules and to communicate when he has gotten out of bed for the twentieth time that night.

To stop a tot from going overboard (and keep him from getting hurt if he does manage to scramble out), you can:

- Lower the mattress as low as it goes.

- Put pillows on the ground around the crib to cushion falls.

- Remove any large toys or stuffed animals from the crib that he may be able to step up on.

- When your child does get out, return him to the crib with minimal interaction and say, "No climbing."

- Stay nearby at bedtime and peek through the door. If you see your child start to raise his leg say, "No climbing."

- Get a mesh crib tent. Put a positive spin on it by decorating it.

- Dress your child in a "sleep sack"; he won't be able to raise his leg over the crib rail.

AGES 2½ TO 5 YEARS OLD
Average sleep for a 3-year-old: 10½ hours at night, 1½ hours during the day (one nap)
Average sleep for a 4-year-old: 11½ hours at night
Average sleep for a 5-year-old: 11 hours at night
Once your child is in preschool, his schedule will be shaped largely

by the hours he's there, when the class has nap time, and other outside factors. That said, there are some things you can (and should) control:

Generally, you want him to **wake up between 6:00 and 7:30 a.m.** (See page 91 of *Trouble Shooting* if your child persistently wakes up before 6:00 a.m.)

Around age 4, most children stop napping. When your preschooler hits this milestone, make sure he still has some **quiet time in the late afternoon** (looking at books in his room, for example), and move his bedtime up by about an hour—i.e., if he had been getting to bed at 8:30 p.m., now he should be in bed by 7:30 p.m.

By age 5, he can probably stay up a little later—until 8:00 p.m.—and he should sleep until around 7:00 a.m. In other words, he should get **11 hours of uninterrupted sleep each night**; adjust your child's exact bed- and wake-up times to coincide with your family schedule and his school-start time.

Also, be aware that preschoolers are very good at hiding when they're sleepy, which can make it tough to get their bedtime just right. Continue to **watch for sleep cues like yawning, eye-rubbing, thumb-sucking, or crankiness**. If your tot gets that cortisol-fueled second wind (meaning you missed his sleep window), start getting him

6:00 a.m.–7:30 a.m.	Wake-up and breakfast.
Midmorning snack	
12:00 p.m.–12:30 p.m.	Lunch.
1:00 a.m.–3:00 p.m.	Nap (if still napping), or quiet time.
Snack	
5:00 p.m.–5:30 p.m.	Dinner.
6:00 p.m.–6:30 p.m.	Start bath.
7:00 p.m.–8:30 p.m.	Bedtime (exact time depending on age and if your child is still taking a nap).

to bed a half-hour or so earlier from now on. Similarly, if he starts nodding off during his bedtime routine or falls asleep the very second you turn out the lights, you're probably putting him to bed too late. Move bedtime earlier by 15 to 30 minutes.

Changes and Challenges: Switching to the Big Bed

Most children move out of the crib between ages 3 and 4. A child is ready to make the switch when:

- he's at least 2 ½ years old.

- he's mastered the skill of putting himself to sleep at bedtime and getting himself back to sleep when he wakes during the night without any help.

- he's climbing out of his crib easily and frequently (see my tips on dealing with a climber on page 25 if you want your tot to stay in his crib longer).

- he *says* he wants a "big boy" bed.

There are different ways to make the transition:

The Cold Turkey Approach—in other words, simply **removing the crib and replacing it with a bed**. If you do this:

- put the new bed where your child's crib was (if the layout of the room allows for it) *or*

- place it in a corner of the room so he still feels safely contained.

- install a guard rail on the side of the bed that's not against a wall.

- arrange a few pillows on the floor in case he tumbles out anyway.

A Note about Toddler Beds: Some families use toddler beds (they're sized to fit a crib mattress) as an interim step, but I don't see a need for it. If your child really wants one, fine, but it's certainly not an essential investment. The one advantage is that they're usually too small for a parent to fit in, so you won't have to deal with being begged to lie down with your child.

The Gradual Approach:

- Start by leaving the crib railing down, with a stool at the side so he can get out by himself.

- Arrange some extra pillows on the floor for safety.

- If you can fit the new bed and the crib in the same room, you can start with reading books on the bed or have him nap in the bed. Then pick the big night where he sleeps in the bed at night. Once he's sleeping in his bed for naps and nights, you can remove the crib.

Some other things to keep in mind, no matter how you decide to make the transition:

- Consider putting a gate on the bedroom door, at least at the beginning, as both a training device and a safety measure. The gate delineates boundaries, helping a child understand that he has to stay in his bed. It will also prevent him from wandering around and possibly getting hurt in a dark house in the middle of the night.

- Make sure the room is safety proof now that he can get out of bed unsupervised.

- Let him pick out new sheets or a quilt (or at least give him a choice between two or three sets that meet your aesthetic requirements!).

- Explain the privileges but also review the rules. Make sure he understands that you will still put him to bed, but then he's expected to stay there.

- Be consistent from day one. If your tot gets out of bed, take him right back without any fuss.

- Reward him in the morning for staying in bed: Give him lots of stickers and let him call his grandparents to brag about the new bed.

If you're about to embark on my Sleep Lady® Shuffle or some other major nighttime changes, like taking away a bottle or pacifier, consider whether it would be easier if you kept him in the crib a little longer. It keeps him in a safe and familiar environment while you're changing other aspects of his sleep, and it may be simpler if you don't have to worry about him getting up and out of bed while you're trying to teach him how to sleep in it.

SLEEP-TIGHT TIP

 If you have a new baby on the way and you'll need the crib before you think your toddler will be ready to give it up (even though he meets all the criteria that make it safe for him to do so), make the transition at least two months before the new sibling is due, or four months after he's born. If your older child still isn't ready to give up his crib, borrow one for the baby or buy a safe used one.

CHAPTER THREE

The Sleep Lady® Shuffle

 For children over 6 months, a central aspect of my program is the Sleep Lady Shuffle. Think of it as a kind of weaning for sleep: You're easing your child from bad habits, like needing to be nursed to sleep, and establishing good sleep practices, like self-soothing—without resorting to techniques that may be hard for you to stomach (like letting your child "cry it out") or that don't fit in with your lifestyle (such as bringing your baby into your bed).

The Shuffle can work for kids of all ages, but is most often used for babies and toddlers (you'll find guidelines for using it with older children in beds in Chapter 9 page 76). Here's how it works:

- Start at bedtime, after a good day of napping. Go through a nice, calming bedtime routine—nursing or bottle-feeding, a song, etc.—in the child's room with a light on.

- Turn *off* the lights (a dim nightlight is okay) and place your child in her crib drowsy but awake. For many children this may be the first time they're put down while aware of what's happening, and they may well protest with crying and tears.

- For the first three nights, position a chair beside the crib where you can sit and easily comfort and reassure your child (see "Guidelines for Sitting by the Crib").

Guidelines for Sitting by the Crib

1. **Don't try to make your child lie down (if she's old enough to stand).** You won't win! Pat the mattress and encourage her to lie down. When she does you can touch her and say soothing things like "Sh, sh," "Night-night," "It's okay," and so forth.

2. **You can stroke, sh-sh, pat, rub, etc. your child *intermittently* through the rails of the crib**—but not constantly—until she falls asleep. She'll expect the same treatment when she wakes up in the middle of the night. Take your hand away when you notice your child starting to fall asleep.

3. ***You* must control the touch.** In other words, don't let your child fall asleep holding your finger or hand, because when you move she'll wake up and you'll have to start all over. Pat or stroke a different part of her body.

4. **It's okay to pick up your child if she becomes hysterical.** Stay in her room and hold her until she settles down. Be careful that you don't hold your child for so long that she falls asleep in your arms. Once she's calm, give her a kiss, put her back in her crib, and sit down in the chair. One note: If you pick up your child and she *immediately* quiets down, then you've been "had." Instead of you training her to sleep, she trained you to pick her up. Next time, wait a bit longer. You'll know within a night or two whether picking her up helps or further stimulates her.

5. **Stay beside her crib until she's sound asleep at bedtime, and during all night awakenings during the first three days of the Shuffle.** If you rush out of the room the minute your baby closes her eyes, chances are she'll wake up and you'll have to start over again. (This is especially true of children over a year old.)

6. **Return to your Shuffle position and follow these rules each time the baby wakes during the first three nights** (as long as you and your pediatrician have decided to end night feeding). Go to the crib, give him a kiss, encourage him to lie down if necessary, and sit in the chair. Do this at each awakening until 6:00 a.m.

- Every three days you will move the chair farther from your baby's crib (see "Recommended Chair Positions").

- During the Shuffle, when you're no longer by your child's bedside, but are sitting by the door, for example, and your child wakes at midnight—go over to her crib, reassure her, give her a kiss, encourage her to lie down (if she's standing), and return to your chair by the door. You may go back over to the crib to pick her up if she becomes hysterical, but hold her only until she's calm, then put her back in the crib and return to your chair.

Recommended Chair Positions

Position 1 Beside the crib

Position 2 Halfway between the crib and the door (if the room is very small or the crib is close to the door, you should instead go ahead to Position 3 by the door). For children in beds skip this chair position.

Position 3 Beside the door inside the room.

Position 4 In the hallway, where your baby can still see you.

Position 5 In the hallway, out of your child's view but where she can still hear you.

Within a couple of weeks, you'll be able to put your baby down to sleep, say, "Good night," and leave the room knowing that she'll happily and easily get herself to sleep without needing your help.

A Note about Multiple Caregivers during Sleep Training:

As I've said, it's fine for parents to establish somewhat different bedtime routines (maybe Mom isn't into singing but Dad's a pro at lullabies, or Dad would rather tell a story than read a board book). Even so, the bedtime routines of a baby's various caregivers (including babysitters, nannies, and family members who're around on a regular basis) should at least be similar. But while you're sleep training, it's generally a good idea to have one parent in charge each night. If, for example, you're on day five of the Sleep Lady® Shuffle, and Dad is sitting in a chair halfway across the room, Mom shouldn't switch places with him after ten minutes. This just stimulates and confuses the child. That said, it's not necessary to have one person "on duty" all night for middle-of-the-night awakenings. Some couples split the night up or trade off because of their own sleep needs and body rhythms, Mom taking, say, midnight to 3:00 a.m. and Dad taking 3:00 to 6:00 a.m.

Virginia, age 6½ months

CHAPTER FOUR

Nap Coaching

 If your child is over 6 months and you need to get his daytime sleep on track, **start on day two, or the morning after the first night, of the Sleep Lady® Shuffle. Some things to keep in mind:**

- **Make sure you're timing your child's naps correctly,** based on his age (as laid out in Chapter 2). Also, be aware of his sleep cues and windows of wakefulness.

- Do an abbreviated version of his bedtime routine, then put your baby in his crib drowsy but awake. Sit beside the crib and soothe him just as you would during the night. **Try for one hour to get him to sleep.**

- **Try the nap in the crib twice a day (and once a day if your child is on one nap) before going to a "backup nap plan":** You go to a backup plan if you check your sleep log around 2:00 or 3:00 p.m. and realize that your child hasn't had enough day sleep. You want to make sure that he sleeps one way or another for a decent interval before the afternoon is over, so that you're not set up for a bad night. A backup nap can take place in the car, stroller, swing, or carrier, but try to make it different from a habit you've been trying to break. For instance, if you've been working on ending co-sleeping at night, don't put him in your bed for his backup nap. Try a car ride or walk in the stroller instead. Ideally, the backup nap will last at least 45 minutes, and your child will be awake by 4:30 p.m. so that he's ready to sleep at his regular bedtime.

- **No naps before 8:00 a.m.**—even if your child has been up since 5:00! It will throw off the entire day and ingrain in him the habit of getting up too early. I realize this is a tricky dance and your child may get overtired, but it's worth it in the long run.

- Your baby's **morning nap should be no longer then 1½ hours**. Wake him if need be. I know this goes against the rule of "never wake a sleeping baby," but I only want you to do it for the morning nap to help regulate your baby's sleeping times.

- Follow the same chair positions for naps as you do at night.

- If you have an older child who can't be left alone while you sit in your baby's room, you can do **timed checks—looking in on your baby at regular intervals.** Base the timing on your little one's temperament and be consistent. If you have no idea where to start, then try checking on him every seven minutes, slowly increasing the time. When you go to his crib, be reassuring but quick. You'll defeat the purpose if you pat him until he's asleep during your crib-side check.

The Three Most Common Nap-Coaching Snafus and How to Handle Them

1. **Your child doesn't go to sleep for the entire hour**. Do your dramatic wake-up routine (open the blinds, sing "Good morning or afternoon, Baby!") and take your child out of bed. Since he hasn't had a morning nap, he won't be able to last (or wait) until the

afternoon for his next nap. Watch his cues: If he starts yawning, dozing while you feed him, etc.—even if it's just 45 minutes after you got him out of his crib—go ahead and try for a nap again.

2. **Your child only sleeps for 45 minutes in the morning.** This is the bare minimum for a nap. If he wakes up happy and seemingly refreshed, that's okay, but be aware that he might be ready for his afternoon siesta sooner rather than later (after two hours awake rather than three). Watch for drowsy cues so you don't miss his sleep window. In addition, do all you can to make sure that the afternoon nap doesn't get cut short. I find that when babies wake up happy after a 45-minute morning nap, they often don't wake up happy and refreshed after a 45-minute afternoon nap. If your child wakes up after 45 minutes from his later nap, use the Shuffle techniques to get him back to sleep (try for at least 30 minutes if you can).

3. **Your child naps for *less than* 45 minutes.** This is a "disaster nap." When a child sleeps for fewer than 45 minutes, he doesn't go through a complete sleep cycle; technically, his wide-eyed state is really a partial arousal, not true wakefulness. So here's the tough message: I want you to go to him and **do the Shuffle for an hour**—what I call "the longest hour."

Here's an example: You put your child in his crib at 9:00 a.m., he conks out at 9:30, but only sleeps until 10:00. You go in and work on getting him back to sleep—which he does, thankfully, by 10:30, after just half an hour. But he only sleeps for 20 minutes. Chances are the negative voice in you is going to say, "I can't believe the Sleep Lady® told me to do that! He cried more than he slept. What's the point of that?" But think about it: Your baby did it! He put himself back to sleep after a partial arousal from a nap—one of the hardest things to do. Going forward, he'll begin to get back to sleep more quickly and will snooze for longer, if you stick with it.

When Your Daytime Caregiver Balks at Nap Coaching

Sometimes nannies, sitters, daycare providers, and even family members aren't comfortable with letting a baby cry (even when they're right by the child's side), or don't want to deal with the tedium of spending up to an hour doing the Shuffle after a too-short snooze. If you run up against this kind of resistance, no matter how carefully you've explained the principles of sleep science:

- Ask the caregiver to focus on "filling the sleep tank" as best she can using whatever sleep crutch she's always used before— in other words, have her at least make sure that your child meets the age-appropriate amount of daytime sleep no matter what it takes. If, for example, she generally rocks your baby to sleep, then have her continue to do this when putting your baby down for naps. Tell her to rock him back to sleep if he wakes before 45 minutes so that he's not having disaster naps all day long. As long as *you* don't rock him to sleep during the day or night, this can work.

- In the meantime, you should work on nighttime sleep and weekend naps. When you're fairly confident that your child has learned to get himself to sleep, talk to your caregiver again. Explain what your baby has accomplished, and ask her to work with you by putting your baby down drowsy but awake. If your baby is in a daycare center, perhaps the provider would be willing to put him down in the sleep area a few minutes before she brings in the rest of the babies.

- Note that at some point during your child's overall sleep training, your caregiver's go-to-sleep techniques may stop working. Often I find that, once a child learns to put himself to sleep, the original sleep crutch stops working. Don't panic: This is a good sign; and it also means your sitter will have to join the sleep-coaching team!

And if you or your partner can't deal with nap coaching at the same time you're focused on night sleep coaching, feel free to use backup measures or temporary fixes to get your child some daytime sleep, preferably at predictable times. Nurse him, pat him, swing him, do what you have to do. But don't give up on naps completely or convince yourself that he doesn't need them. As nighttime sleep improves, the daytime sleep might fall into place on its own. It not, take a deep breath and try the training again in another month or two **or** when your backup measures stop working—whichever comes first.

Some Important Things to Keep in Mind

- The morning nap develops first and is easier for a child to achieve than the afternoon nap, so don't miss this opportunity.

- The afternoon nap is more stubborn, so don't get discouraged!

- Look at your sleep log around 2:00 or 3:00 p.m. and decide if you will need to go for a backup nap.

- You will be tied to the house during the nap-coaching process. If you feel like all you're doing all day is trying to get your child to go to sleep, then you're doing everything right! Hang in there. *You can do this!*

Max, age 8 months

CHAPTER FIVE

How to Eliminate Nighttime Feeding during the Shuffle

One of my hardest tasks is convincing parents that most healthy 6- to 8-month-old babies on a normal growth curve don't need to eat at night. Even a smart, thoughtful mom who knows this in her head may still have a fear of letting her child go hungry—especially when that child is waking in the middle of the night. Check with your pediatrician to make sure that your little one doesn't have a health issue that would make it necessary for her to eat during the night; but the overwhelming odds are that the main reason an older baby still gets up in search of breast or bottle is that sucking is the only way she knows how to get back to sleep. Don't be hard on yourself if your child has developed this habit. It's very common—because it works!—but it's time to break the habit.

Families I've worked with have tried all of the techniques outlined *below* for eliminating nighttime feedings; make the choice that best matches your child's temperament. I suggest starting with the most gradual one, Method A, but if you feel confident that B or C makes more sense for you and your baby, go ahead and start with that. In any case, please read through this entire chapter; many of the tips can be applied to any of the strategies.

Whatever approach you take, it will be easier if you try to reset your baby's hunger clock so that she takes in more calories by day and therefore isn't looking around for more at night. I know some babies, even this young, who do a remarkable job of snacking all day so they can feast all night.

SLEEP-TIGHT TIP

Whatever night-weaning-method you choose *be consistent and stick with it!*

Start by reviewing her daytime feeding schedule and keeping a written log of her diet for a week. Go over it with her doctor to make sure she's getting the right mix of breast milk and/or formula and solids. Try to nurse or bottle-feed her in a quiet, dim place without television, phone, or other distractions *so that she can focus on taking a full feeding*. This advice holds true during growth spurts too. She may need an occasional night feeding mid-spurt, but by enhancing her daytime feeding, you'll minimize the nighttime ones.

Once you and your pediatrician have agreed that your baby does not need any feeding during an 11-hour period at night, then choose one of the methods that follow, and decide how many nights you'll keep it up before completely eliminating the nighttime meal. Ideally you want to be done with the process within a week, so set a specific night ahead of time as the night you will not feed her.

Method A: The Taper-off Technique

If you're nursing, gradually cut down the amount of time your baby is at the breast. For example, if she usually feeds for 20 minutes, let her go for only 15. Cut back every few nights until she's ready to give it up, or until you're down to 5 minutes: At that point, it's just a tease and it's time to stop altogether. Make sure you unlatch her when she finishes eating heartily, even if it's sooner than the amount of time you've allotted; don't let her just gently suckle and doze. Get her back to bed while she's drowsy but awake.

If you're bottle-feeding, you can decrease the amount of formula she gets by a few ounces every few nights. When you get to two ounces, it's time to stop. An alternative is to gradually dilute the formula until it gets so watery she decides it's not worth getting up for. I usually find reducing the total ounces in each bottle every few nights works best.

Method B: The Four-Night Phase-out

Whether you're breastfeeding or giving a bottle, feed your baby just *once* during the night for three nights; it's best to set a rule for when you'll give her that single snack, so you can either:

- feed her the first time she wakes after a set time such as midnight, or

- the first time she wakes as long as it's been *at least four hours* since she last ate, or

- a *dream feed*, in which you wake her for her final feeding right before you go to bed.

Only feed her once at night, and not again until at least 6:00 a.m. when you can both start your day. If she wakes at other times sit by her crib and offer physical and verbal reassurance. Follow the "Guidelines for Sitting by the Crib," outlined on page 31.

On the fourth night don't feed her at all. Remember she has had three nights to get used to receiving fewer calories at night. Usually parents will move their seat away from the crib on the fourth night of the Shuffle, but we're going to modify it for this night-weaning. So on the fourth night when she wakes up, sit next to her crib for an additional night. Comfort her from your chair as you did at bedtime. Don't pick her up unless she's hysterical, and then hold her only briefly. If you breastfeed exclusively, it may help to put Dad on night-duty: Since he can't nurse, your baby might adjust to the no-night-feeding routine more quickly.

Important Note: Let's say you've decided that you'll feed your baby the first time she wakes after midnight. If you find yourself sitting with her and doing the Shuffle from 11:00 p.m. until midnight while she fusses, don't pick her up and feed her a minute after the clock strikes 12:00. Wait until she goes back to sleep and then wakes up again—even if she only dozes for half an hour. You don't want to send the message that crying for an hour will yield a feeding.

Method C: Cold Turkey

You can simply stop offering your baby a breast or a bottle when she wakes at night. Go to her cribside as outlined in the Shuffle. Just make sure you and your partner are on the same page in this decision. If Mom has been breastfeeding, consider having Dad handle all middle-of-the-night wake-ups, since your child knows that he can't give in and nurse her.

REDUCING THE NUMBER OF FEEDINGS AT NIGHT *WITHOUT* ELIMINATING THEM ALL TOGETHER:

Let's say you and your pediatrician think your baby still needs to eat at night, or you want to merely reduce nighttime feedings but aren't ready to cut them out altogether; follow the first step of Method B and restrict meals to *once* a night. Feed your child quickly, and avoid other interactions that will encourage her to stay up and play or cling to you.

Noah, age 10 months

CHAPTER SIX

Putting an End to Co-Sleeping

 Many families who co-sleep are doing it *because* their child is unable to put himself to sleep without a parent lying next to him, holding him, or nursing him to sleep—not because it's part of their parenting style. (Even if you want to co-sleep, you should still teach your child to soothe himself to sleep.)

After a baby has been in your bed for months (or years!), I suggest making changes in several stages, described in detail *below*, over several weeks (though not every family needs to go through every step). If your child is old enough, prepare him by talking through the imminent change. Even a 1-year-old can comprehend more than you realize, and certainly from 18 months or so kids can understand a good deal. Let your tot know what's coming and make it sound enticing and exciting. For an older child, sticker charts and rewards are great incentives.

Stage One: Daytime and Playtime

Get your child used to his room when he is awake and in daylight. In fact, he shouldn't just be used to it, he should *like* it. Play with him there, change him there, hug him and kiss him there. If he needs some incentives to venture into an unfamiliar room, buy him some fun new toys or check some books and tapes out of the library. **(You can skip this stage if your child is already playing in his room and/or napping there.)**

Stage Two: Napping

If your child is not already napping in his bedroom, start now. Spend a week or two getting him accustomed to napping in his own crib or bed during the day, before you make the nighttime transition. Lie down *with him* in his room for two or three days if your intuition tells you he needs that extra assistance. If he has trouble falling asleep in his room and you don't want to lie down with him, sit with him for the next few days but try to be a fairly neutral presence. Calm and soothe him but don't let him constantly engage you, or all the inter-action will be an excuse for him not to sleep. After a few days, try the Sleep Lady® Shuffle for nap training. If you do, note that it's up to you whether you want to address the napping first, or napping and night-time sleep simultaneously—it doesn't matter if you are sitting in ex-actly the same position day and night at this point.

Instead of the Shuffle, you have the option of trying to settle your child for a nap with his lovey and then leaving the room and checking on him every five minutes if he's crying. If that feels too abrupt to you, remember that either approach is fine, and that you should choose the one that feels best for you and suits your child. Read the chapter for your child's age for details on the Shuffle and nap coaching.

Stage Three: Co-Sleeping in Your Child's Room

When you or your child is ready for night-training—and it will be clear; we're talking days or weeks, not months—you should start the Sleep Lady® Shuffle, with one extra preliminary phase: **Spend up to three nights sleeping in his room with him to create a bridge be-tween the family bed and independent sleep.** Throw a mattress on the floor, drag in the guest bed, pile up some sleeping bags, whatever is safe and comfortable for both of you to sleep on.

Stage Four: Start the Sleep Lady® Shuffle

Depending on whether you are transitioning your child to a crib or bed, read either Chapter 8 or 9 on "Implementing Your Plan" for more details.

Once you've gone through your usual bedtime routine, put your child in his bed or crib. Sit next to the crib or bed to soothe him. Pat him or rub his back intermittently, but don't relent and bring him into your bed or the makeshift bed on the floor. Stay next to his crib or bed until he is completely asleep.

You can sleep in his room on the makeshift bed if that will make you more comfortable and consistent, but only for two or three nights. Any longer, and he'll have an even harder time adjusting when you leave. If your child is in a bed, and he gets out and tries to join you on the floor, simply put him back immediately without a word. If he does this repeatedly or if you wake up at night and find he's in bed with you, skip ahead to the Shuffle step where you sit in a chair and stop sleeping in his room.

Each time your child wakes during the night, return to his bedside to offer physical and verbal reassurance until he goes back to sleep. Sit

next to your child's crib or bed for three nights to soothe him. Every three nights move a little farther away so that he can gradually fall asleep more independently. Move across the room, then to the doorway, then out the door into the hall, until finally you're able to leave him alone while still checking on him frequently. (Take a look at the Shuffle overview on pages 30–32 for more details.)

Owen, age 15 months

CHAPTER SEVEN

Creating Your Plan

Now it's time to devise your own sleep-coaching plan! I always encourage parents to *create their plan together and during the waking hours.* Think it through, talk it through, and *write it down.* Putting your plan on paper will ensure that you're both on the same page (literally and figuratively!) and will help you avoid miscommunication. Most important, it will help you be consistent with your child.

Following are sample plans for a 7-month-old in a crib and a 3-year-old in a bed, and after that, there is a blank plan for you to fill in and tear out.

Below is a sample plan for Bridget who is 7 months old and sleeps in a crib.

Our Plan for Bridget

We have met with our pediatrician and have discussed our child's eating, growth, and general health. We have ruled out any potential underlying medical conditions that may be interfering with our child's sleep. Our pediatrician has given us the green light to begin sleep coaching.

After reviewing the sleep averages, we have found that our child requires on average the following amount of sleep:

Total amount of nighttime sleep: **11 hours**
Total amount of daytime sleep: **3.25 hours**
Number of naps: **2 to 3**

After reviewing my child's eating and sleep logs over the last few days, we believe his/her natural bedtime window is: **around 7:00 p.m.**

We will be working toward an approximate eating and sleeping schedule as outlined below:

6:00 a.m.–7:30 a.m.	Wake-up range
Breakfast or feeding	
8:30 a.m.–9:00 a.m.	Nap (or within 2 hours of waking but not before 8:00 a.m.), 1½ hours max
Lunch or feeding	
Around 1:00 p.m.	Nap (or within 2–3 hours of waking from her first nap but asleep within 3 hours)
Snack	
5:00 p.m.–5:30 p.m.	Dinner or feeding
6:00 p.m.–6:30 p.m.	Start bath/bedtime routine (depends on whether it is a bath night)
6:45 p.m.	Feeding
7:00 p.m.	Lights out and in bed

Our bedtime routine will include the following:

1. bath or wash up

2. massage

3. nurse with a night-light on

4. short song or book

5. into crib awake

If applicable, we have created a sleep manner sticker chart with the following manners:

OUR BEDTIME PLAN:

- Dad will sit by the crib until Bridget falls asleep.

- Dad has reviewed all the rules of the Shuffle outlined on pages 30-32.

- Dad will decide when it is appropriate to pick up Bridget to calm her and will determine if it helps her.

- Mom will not coach Dad from the doorway and will support his efforts knowing that he loves Bridget and is a caring father to her.

- Mom and Dad agree that learning to put yourself to sleep is an essential life skill and that it is one of our tasks as parents to teach Bridget.

OUR CHAIR POSITIONS WILL BE AS FOLLOWS:

- Nights 1–3 by the crib

- Nights 4–6 by door (her room is small and her crib is near the door so a halfway position isn't necessary)

- Nights 7–10 hallway in view. She can see us from her crib.

- Nights 11–13 hallway out of view with her door open a crack to a few inches

- Nights 14 and on—leave and "sh" intermittently from doorway if still necessary

OUR NIGHTTIME STRATEGY:

- We and the pediatrician agree that Bridget needs one feeding during an 11–12 hr. night.

- We will feed her at the first waking after midnight and then not until 6 a.m. the earliest and then we will start our day.

- For this one feeding Mom will go in, change her diaper and nurse Bridget and place her back in the crib. Mom will unlatch her once she is done with her feeding and not allow her to suckle back to sleep.

- Dad will go in and sit next to Bridget's crib at each waking before and after the feeding and follow the Shuffle rules outlined on pages 30–32.

- We will not bring Bridget out of her room to start the day before 6 a.m.

- We will not bring Bridget back in to Mom and Dad's bed.

Example of nighttime strategy if Bridget did NOT need a feeding during the night and needed to be weaned from several night feedings:

- We and the pediatricians agree that Bridget is a healthy weight and does not need to receive calories during an 11–12 hr period at night.

- We have decided to wean her from her night feedings over 3 nights.

- For 3 nights we will feed her at the first waking after midnight and then not until 6 a.m. the earliest and then we will start our day.

- For this one feeding Mom will go in, change her diaper and nurse Bridget and place her back in the crib. Mom will unlatch her once she is done with her feeding and not allow her to suckle back to sleep.

- Dad will go in and sit next to Bridget's crib at each waking before and after the feeding and follow the Shuffle rules outlined on pages 30–32.

- We will not bring Bridget out of her room to start the day before 6 a.m.

- We will not bring Bridget back in to Mom and Dad's bed.

- On the fourth night we will not feed Bridget during the night and will treat every waking the same.

- Mom and Dad have decided to split up the night as follows:

- When Bridget wakes between bedtime-1:00 a.m. Mom will go in and sit by the crib and follow the rules outlined on page 31.

- When Bridget wakes between 1:00 a.m.-6:00 a.m. Dad will go in and sit by the crib and follow the rules outlined on page 31.

- If she wakes before 6:00 a.m. and does NOT go back to sleep by 6:00 a.m. we will leave the room and come back in and do "dramatic wake up."

OUR CHAIR POSITIONS WILL BE AS FOLLOWS:

- Nights 1-4 by the crib—we will sit by the crib an extra night on the first night she goes without a feeding all night.

- Nights 5-7 by door (Her room is small and her crib is near the door so a halfway position is not necessary.)

- Nights 8-11 hallway in view. She can see us from her crib.

- Nights 12-14 hallway out of view with her door open a crack to a few inches

- Nights 15 and on—leave and "sh" intermittently from doorway if still necessary

OUR NAP PLAN:

- We have decided to start the nap coaching process also.

- We will start the morning after the first night of sleep coaching.

We will be using the flexible schedule we outlined above. We have reviewed the nap coaching on pages 34–35.

OUR SHORTENED PRE-NAP ROUTINE WILL BE:

1. pull the shades down in room, change diaper

2. comfort nurse with light on if at home

3. short book

OUR BACKUP NAP PLAN IS:

We will take Bridget for a stroller or car ride on weekends when she is home. Our goal is for her to nap at least **45 minutes or** be awake by 4:30 p.m.

OUR NAP PLAN AT HOME:

We will nap coach Bridget in her crib on the weekends or other weekdays we are home.

OUR DAY CARE PROVIDER HAS AGREED TO THE FOLLOWING:

She cannot nap coach our child since she has other children to care for but she is willing to make sure Bridget gets 3-3½ hours of day naps even if she has to sleep in the swing or stroller. We shared with her Bridget's schedule and average windows of wakefulness and she is willing to work with us on the timing of her day naps.

We're ready to go! We have blocked out three weeks of our schedule and are dedicating ourselves to improving our child's sleep habits! There is sleep for all at the end of the tunnel!

Below is a sample plan for Max, a 3-year-old who sleeps in a bed.

Our Plan for Max

We have met with our pediatrician and have discussed our child's eating, growth, and general health. We have ruled out any potential underlying medical conditions that may be interfering with our child's sleep. Our pediatrician has given us the green light to begin sleep coaching.

After reviewing the sleep averages, we have found that our child requires on average the following amount of sleep:

Total amount of nighttime sleep:	**10½ hours**
Total amount of daytime sleep:	**1½ hours**
Number of naps:	**1**

After reviewing my child's eating and sleep logs over the last few days we believe his/her natural bedtime window is: **7:30–8:00 p.m.**

We will be working toward an approximate eating and sleeping schedule as outlined below:

6:00 a.m.–7:30 a.m.	Wake-up range. Max tends to wake at 6:30 a.m. and acts rested with 10½ hours of sleep at night.
Breakfast	
12 noon	Lunch.
Around 1:00 p.m.	Nap. We will wake him after 1½ hours since if he sleeps longer it is harder for him to go to bed on time.
Snack	

5:00 p.m.–5:30 p.m.	Dinner or feeding
6:30 p.m.	Start bath/bedtime routine (depends on whether it is a bath night)
7:45 p.m.	Lights out and in bed

Our bedtime routine will include the following:

1. bath or wash up

2. put on pajamas and pick out 2 books

3. read books

4. share "3 things I liked about my day"

5. review of sleep manner chart, kisses, and lights out

We have created a sleep manner sticker chart with the following manners:

- cooperates at bedtime

- lies quietly in bed

- goes to sleep without Mommy or Daddy lying down with him

- puts self back to sleep quietly during the night without Mommy or Daddy lying down with him

- stays in bed quietly until the wake-up music comes on

OUR BEDTIME PLAN:

- Mom and Dad will have a family meeting and discuss with Max the sleep manners that are expected of him. We will also tell him that we will no longer be lying down with him at bedtime or during the night but that we will stay with him while he learns to put himself to sleep.

- Mom and Dad will alternate nights and will discuss this prior to bedtime.

- On the first night Mom will review Max's sleep manners before turning off the lights.

- Mom will sit by Max's bed at bedtime until he falls asleep.

- Once lights are out there will be little engagement or discussions with Max. We will only agree to cover him up two times and then he will have to do it himself.

- Mom and Dad have reviewed all the rules of the Shuffle outlined on pages 30-32.

- Mom will move away from the bedside if Max continues to put his legs on her or tries to put his head on her lap and will not be redirected.

- Mom will hug Max to calm him down if needed but will not lay down with him.

- Mom and Dad agree to be a united front and consistent with Max knowing that this will help Max.

- We acknowledge that changing sleep habits in a 3-year-old can take longer.

- Mom and Dad agree that learning to put yourself to sleep is an essential life skill and that it is one of our tasks as parents to teach Max.

OUR CHAIR POSITIONS WILL BE AS FOLLOWS:

- Nights 1-3 by the bed

- Nights 4-6 by door. If Max continues to get out of the bed when we are sitting at the door we will stand, count to 3 and say, "Max I will not sit in your room unless you stay in your bed quietly. I will count to 3 and if you are not in your bed I will leave and shut the door." If we have to leave and shut the door we will count to 10 and open the door and tell Max, "If you get in your bed I will come and sit in your room." We will say this in a calm but firm voice. We will do this as often as necessary until he gets back into the bed.

- Nights 7-10 hallway in view. He can see us from his bed. We realize this may be the most difficult phase for Max. We will respond the same way as outlined above if he gets out of the bed. We may also consider putting up a gate until his sleep manners improve.

- Nights 11-13 hallway out of view with his door open a crack to a few inches. We will use our voice intermittently to reassure him of our presence if necessary.

- Nights 14 and on—leave and do "job checks." We will tell him that we will check on him after we brush our teeth, for example. We will stay upstairs in our room for a few nights until he is asleep and then progress to going downstairs.

OUR NIGHTTIME STRATEGY:

- Each time Max wakes and gets out of his bed we will take his hand and walk him back to his bed.

- Each time he wakes up before 6:00 a.m. we will tell him calmly that "Your wake-up music is not on, which means its still nighttime so you must go back to sleep in your bed."

- We will sit by his bed until he is asleep for the first three nights and follow the above chair positions.

OUR NAP PLAN:

- We agree that Max still needs one daytime nap.

- We have decided to start the nap-coaching process also.

- We will start the afternoon after the first night of sleep coaching.

We will be using the flexible schedule we outlined above. We have reviewed the nap coaching on pages 34–35.

OUR SHORTENED PRE-NAP ROUTINE WILL BE:

1. pull shades down and review sleep manners for nap

2. read books

3. lights out

OUR BACK UP NAP PLAN IS:

We will take Max for a car ride on weekends and when he is

home during the week. Our goal is for him to nap at least 45 minutes or be awake by 4:00 p.m.

OUR NAP PLAN AT HOME:

- During the weekends or days Max is not in school he will nap in his bed.

- Nap time will be between 12 noon to 1 p.m. like in preschool.

OUR CHILDCARE PROVIDER HAS AGREED TO THE FOLLOWING:

Max is in all-day preschool three days a week. He usually lies quietly in a cot. Preschool has agreed to wake him up after 1 ½ hours of sleep.

We're ready to go! We have blocked out three weeks of our schedule and are dedicating ourselves to improving our child's sleep habits! There is sleep for all at the end of the tunnel!

Our Plan for _____

(your child's name here)

We have met with our pediatrician and have discussed our child's eating, growth, and general health. We have ruled out any potential underlying medical conditions that may be interfering with our child's sleep. Our pediatrician has given us the green light to begin sleep coaching.

After reviewing the sleep averages, we have found that our child requires on average the following amount of sleep:

Total amount of nighttime sleep: _____
Total amount of daytime sleep: _____
Number of naps: _____

After reviewing my child's eating and sleep logs over the last few days we believe his/her natural bedtime window is: _____ p.m.

We will be working toward an approximate eating and sleeping schedule as outlined below:

6:00 a.m.–7:30 a.m.   Wake-up range

Breakfast or feeding

Window of wakefulness   _____

_____a.m. nap   Length min. and max._____

Lunch or feeding

Window of wakefulness   _____

_____ p.m. nap

Window of wakefulness to bedtime_____

Snack

Optional third nap? _____

_____ p.m.   Dinner or feeding

_____ p.m.   Start bath/bedtime routine

                                         Feeding (if age appropriate)

_____ p.m.   Lights out and in bed

OUR BEDTIME ROUTINE WILL INCLUDE THE FOLLOWING:

1. _____
2. _____
3. _____
4. _____
5. _____

If applicable, we have created a sleep manner sticker chart with the following manners:

OUR BEDTIME PLAN:

_____
_____
_____
_____
_____
_____

OUR CHAIR POSITIONS WILL BE AS FOLLOWS:

_____

_____

_____

_____

_____

_____

OUR NIGHTTIME STRATEGY:

Will you be feeding your child during the night?
If yes, outline the feeding plan and who will be doing it.

_____

_____

_____

_____

_____

_____

OUR NAP PLAN:

_____

_____

_____

_____

_____

_____

We will be using the flexible schedule we outlined above.
We have reviewed "Nap Coaching" on page 34–35.

We will begin nap coaching the morning after our first evening of
sleep coaching or _____.

Our shortened pre-nap routine will be:

1. _____

2. _____

3. _____

OUR BACK UP NAP PLAN IS:

_____

_____

_____

_____

_____

_____

OUR NAP PLAN AT HOME:

_____

_____

_____

_____

_____

_____

OUR DAYCARE PROVIDER HAS AGREED TO THE FOLLOWING:

_____

_____

_____

_____

_____

_____

We're ready to go! We have blocked out three weeks of our schedule and are dedicating ourselves to improving our child's sleep habits! There is sleep for all at the end of the tunnel!

CHAPTER EIGHT

Implementing Your Plan: Step–by–Step Shuffle Outline for a Baby or a Child in a Crib

Nights One through Three

Once bath, stories, bottle/nursing, and songs are over, sit in a chair right **next to your baby's crib.** If she cries or fusses, you can stroke or pat her. It's also important that *you* control physical contact: Rather than let your child hold your finger, you should pat her. Take care not to touch her constantly, though (tempting as it will be!). You don't want to swap one negative association, like rocking, for another, like your constant caress or the sound of your voice. Another reason to keep touch to a minimum: On day four you'll be moving your chair away from the side of the crib and frequent contact won't be possible.

Try not to pick her up—but if she's extremely upset go ahead and do it, over the crib if possible. Hold her until she's calm but keep the cuddle brief. Put her down again while she's still awake. You can sing during the get-ready-for-bed stage, but once it's time for sleep, you're better off making soothing "sh-sh" sounds. You might want to try closing your eyes. It will be easier not to talk to her, and it also conveys the message that it's time to sleep. Don't stimulate her—bore her. Stay there until she falls asleep.

When your child wakes up at night during the Shuffle (as she will in the beginning), return to the chair next to her crib and sooth her. You can initially go over to her cribside and quickly calm and caress her and encourage her to lie down (if she's sitting up or standing), before

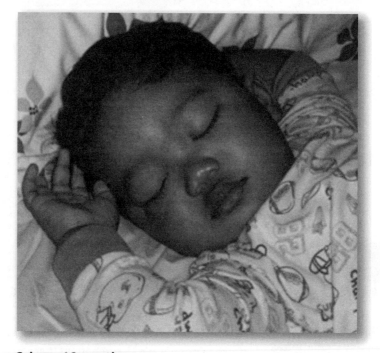

Cai age 16 months

you settle back down in your chair. Stay there until she goes back to sleep. Do this for each waking until 6:00 a.m. (the earliest) when you can both start your day.

If your child has a particularly rough night, don't stop the sleep training. But you may need to let her nap more for a day so she doesn't get impossibly overtired and make the next night even more of a challenge. Provide the extra nap-time within the sample timelines outlined in Chapter 2. Let's say that your 8-month-old has been up since 5:00 a.m. On a normal day, she would start her nap at around 9:00 a.m., but on this day, she'll be too tired to stay awake until 9:00. Don't force it, let her nap at 8:00 a.m. at the earliest—but don't throw her schedule completely out of whack by letting her nap at 6:30 a.m. If she takes a third little nap in late afternoon, that's fine. Or if she naps a half-hour longer than usual, that's fine too. Similarly, if your preschooler normally naps from 1:00 p.m. to 3:00 p.m., it's okay to let her sleep until 4:00 p.m. if she needs it after a hard night or a too early morning—but don't let her snooze all the way until dinner or nap before noon.

Another way of handling a temporary sleep deficit is to put your child to bed a little earlier than usual for a few nights. In short, watch her, trust yourself, and make some commonsense adjustments, but keep them within the basic framework of an age-appropriate schedule.

NIGHTS ONE THROUGH THREE REMINDERS

- Make sure your child gets good naps on the day of your first night of the Shuffle. Look at the nap averages for your child's age in Chapter 2.

- Create your nap time, bedtime, and nighttime sleep plan on pages 59–62.

- Keep a sleep log.

- Plan an early enough bedtime. Watch her sleepy cues and the clock. Do the math backward. For example, a typical 2-year-old needs 11 hours of sleep at night. If her average wake-up time is 7:00 a.m. then she should be *asleep* by 8:00 p.m.

- Focus on what your plan is for the **first night**. Discuss it with the other parent so you are a united front. Split the night up, take turns every other night, or decide who is going to get up for which awakenings.

- Nurse or bottle-feed with the light on. You *don't* want to give the message that "the way we go to sleep at night is to suckle to sleep or get very drowsy in the dark."

- Drowsy but awake: That means more awake than drowsy. If you help your child get into a *very* drowsy state at bedtime, you'll make it harder for her to go back to sleep when she wakes during the night.

- Your child should be aware that she's being put down, which means she may cry, so be prepared.

- Your first chair position is **by the crib**.

- Be careful not to create a new sleep crutch. For example, don't substitute rocking your baby to sleep with patting her back to sleep. Hint: You know you're patting too much if your baby starts crying when you stop touching her.

- There is no limit on how long you sit by your child's bed. Stay as long as it takes, knowing that you don't want to train her to cry. You also don't want to sneak out too soon. When you do that your child (especially if she's over a year old) will become hypervigilant about your leaving and will be up multiple times checking on you.

- Remember, you *can* pick your child up! You'll know within one to two nights whether it helps.

- Pick up to calm and *not to put to sleep.*

- Each time your child wakes up, go over to her cribside: Assess what she needs, encourage her to lie down, reassure her, and sit in your chair.

- Treat each night awakening the same (if you're not feeding during the night).

- Don't give up until after 6:00 a.m. Then do dramatic wake-up: Leave the room, count to 10, and come back in as if nothing happened!

- Start nap coaching on day two.

Nights Four through Six

Move the chair about halfway to the door. (If the room is very small, or the crib is close to the door, you should skip to the next chair position and **sit by the door in her room**.) Continue the soothing sounds, but stay in the chair as much as you can. Get up to pat or stroke your baby a little if necessary, or make the same soothing sounds as you have the past three nights. Try not to pick her up unless she's hysterical. Stay in the chair halfway to the door until she falls asleep.

When your child wakes up during the night, return to the chair position you were in at bedtime that night and sooth her. You can go over to her cribside initially and quickly calm, caress, and encourage her to lie down (if she's standing or sitting) before you return to your chair by the door. Continue the soothing sounds but stay in the chair as much as you can. Get up to pat or stroke her a little if necessary. Try not to pick her up unless she's hysterical, and if you do pick her up, follow the technique I described for the first three nights. Stay in your chair by the door until she's asleep again.

NIGHTS FOUR THROUGH SIX REMINDERS

- There are still night awakenings, but you will have to move your **chair halfway to the door** on the fourth night.

- Keep a sleep log.

- Put your child into the crib drowsy but awake.

- You may get out of your chair and go to the crib to comfort your child if she becomes hysterical.

- Be careful about an older child's efforts to get you to come to her—like throwing things out of her crib. Set a limit, such as "Lie down, sweetie, and Mommy will get you your binky. But you must lie down." You may also have to limit how many times you will return it. Follow through on whatever you say.

- It's common to see a regression the first night you move your chair farther away.

- Children get ritualized easily. Make changes every three days. Dragging it out makes it harder, not easier, for your baby. Give it more than three days and she'll expect you to stay exactly where you are—and get mad or upset when you try to double that distance.

Night four may be the hardest of these three nights. Stay the course!

Nights Seven through Nine

Move the **chair to the doorway or the doorjamb inside her room**. You should be dimly lit but still in her view. Continue the same soothing techniques from your chair, remembering to intervene as little as possible. Don't worry if she cries a little bit; keep quietly reassuring her. She'll know you're there, and she'll fall asleep.

When your child wakes up during the night, return to the chair position you were in at bedtime that night and sooth her. You can go over to the cribside initially and quickly calm and caress her, and then encourage her to lie down (if she's standing or sitting) before you return to your chair by the door. Continue the soothing sounds but stay in the chair as much as you can. Get up to pat or stroke her a little, if necessary. Try not to pick her up unless she's hysterical, and if you do pick her up, follow the technique I described for the first three nights. Stay in your chair by the door until she falls back to sleep.

NIGHTS SEVEN THROUGH NINE REMINDERS

- On night seven you will move your **chair to the door** inside the room.

- If you have decided to keep bumpers on your crib, it's okay to fold back one side of the bumper so your child can see you.

- Use your voice to reassure her.

- Keep a sleep log.

- You may get out of your chair and go to the crib to comfort your child if she becomes hysterical.

- For all nighttime awakenings, you can go to the cribside initially, see what your baby needs, encourage her to lie down, reassure her, and then go back to your chair by the door.

Nights Ten through Twelve

Move the **chair to the hallway, with the door open enough so your child can still see you from the crib**. The hall should be dimly lit. Stay until she falls asleep.

When your child wakes up during the night, return to the chair position you were in at bedtime that night and sooth her. You can go over to the crib initially and quickly calm and caress her, and encourage her to lie down (if she's standing or sitting) before you return to your chair by the door. Continue the soothing sounds but stay in the chair as much as you can. Get up to pat or stroke her a little if necessary. Try not to pick her up unless she's hysterical, and if you do pick her up, follow the technique I described for the first three nights. Stay in your chair in the hallway in view until she's asleep.

NIGHTS TEN THROUGH TWELVE REMINDERS

- Your new chair position on night 10 is the hallway *in view*.

- Your child's bedroom door should be open enough for her to see you from her crib.

- Keep a sleep log.

- This next move on the first night can be difficult because you're not in the room and your child may try every trick she can think of to get you back there. She may throw things or cry until you come; if she's verbal, she might even kick off her blanket and then call you to tuck her back in. Set a limit such as "Mommy will only tuck you in one more time and then you will have to do it yourself." Follow through on whatever you say.

- If you've been consistent up until now you will probably be seeing some improvement—such as fewer, shorter night awakenings. Congratulations.

- Night sleep falls into place on average after 7 to 10 nights (in children under 18 months, two to three weeks in children over 18 months), and naps in two to three weeks. Afternoon naps and early rising can take as long as three to four weeks to improve.

Night Thirteen and Beyond

By now your baby is probably falling asleep and staying asleep on her own. Your last step is to give her a chance to do this without your presence. It may seem like a huge leap, but it's not so big for her. After all, she's had nearly two weeks of preparation! Move farther down the hall, so that you're **out of view but your child can hear you**. You can keep making "sh-sh" sounds—not constantly, but often enough to let her know that you're close by and responsive. If she cries, check on her from the door—don't go over to her crib. Be calm and reassuring. Make some comforting, encouraging sounds to convey that you're not far away and that you know she can put herself to sleep. Your baby really can soothe herself to sleep—if you give her the opportunity.

NIGHT THIRTEEN AND BEYOND REMINDERS

- It's okay to break this step up if it's very upsetting to your child. For instance, you could sit halfway out of view the first night and then move to totally out of view a night or two later.

- Night awakenings have greatly diminished by now and you may only be struggling with early rising. This is especially true if your child had a previous history of early rising. Stay consistent and work on those naps. Early rising can take three to four weeks to improve!

- Remember that early rising is caused by one or more of the following:

  - a too-late bedtime

  - nap deprivation in general

  - a too-large wake-up window between afternoon nap and bedtime. This window should not exceed four hours for a child who is not sleeping through the night yet.

  - putting your child to bed too drowsy at bedtime

- The two hardest parts of sleep coaching are early rising and the stubborn afternoon naps. Stay consistent and these will improve!!

Olivia, age 18 months

CHAPTER NINE

Implementing Your Plan:
Step-by-Step Shuffle Outline
for a Child in a Bed

A child who's old enough to sleep in a big-kid bed is old enough to become vested in improving his own sleep, and can feel proud when he does. Positive reinforcement goes a long way for this age group.

Children who move from the crib too early don't necessarily have the verbal skills to understand big-boy or big-girl bedtime rules (which on average are developed at 2½ years old). That means this process will take longer and you very well may have to install a gate. Be patient and consistent. If your toddler is on a mattress on the floor or in a low toddler bed, sit nearby on the floor, not on a chair.

The Family Meeting

Choose a time when your child is happy and receptive. Sunday morning after pancakes is a lot better than 5:00 p.m. on a weekday when she skipped her nap and is starving for dinner. Tell her that you read a book by the Sleep Lady® and learned about how children can sleep better. That way you can blame me for any changes or rules she doesn't like. For instance, if your child begs you to lie down with her you can say the Sleep Lady® said we can't do that but we can stay with you in your room. Some children get furious with me. "The Sleep Lady® can't come over to play with me!" "I don't like the Sleep Lady®." But when they succeed, when they start feeling good about their new sleep skills, they often want to call me on the phone and tell me how proud they are of themselves! In the back of this workbook is a certificate you can tear out, fill in, and give to your child!

Keep the discussion upbeat and positive. You don't want your child to feel she has a problem, or that she's doing something wrong. Portray it as your problem, your responsibility. "Mommy and Daddy should have helped you learn to put yourself to sleep earlier, and we are sorry we didn't. But the Sleep Lady® helped us understand that and now we are going to help you learn." Explain that children who go to bed without fussing and who sleep all night feel better in the morning and have more fun during the day. Encourage your child to brainstorm about how she can participate, maybe by deciding what she can take into her bed to touch or hug, or what extra game she will get to play in the morning if she uses her good-sleep manners at night. You want her to have a stake in success. You may be surprised at how sensitive children already are to sleep issues, and how quickly they pick up the lingo. Many kids are relieved when parents bring this up. They know that something is wrong, that Mom and Dad are frustrated and want them to sleep differently. They're happy to know you are going to help them fix it.

If you think it will help, you can give your child examples, preferably of an older friend or cousin she looks up to. Say something like, "We're going to teach you how to put yourself to sleep and sleep all night long in your own bed, just like Cousin Johnny and Cousin Jenny and Gramma and Aunt Rachel." Be sure to frame this in a positive way, not one to make your child feel ashamed.

Explain clearly and specifically what changes are coming. "Daddy is not going to lie down with you anymore, but Daddy *will* stay with you until you fall asleep." Or, "If you come to our bed at night, we're going to tell you we love you and take you back into your bed where you can snuggle with your teddy bear." Adapt the script to the appropriate sleep challenge, but you don't have to give a lot more detail. You can introduce the idea of a sticker chart so your child will know exactly what behavior you'll expect.

I strongly encourage you to use what I call **"wake-up music"** or **a light with an attached appliance timer**. You can purchase an inexpensive CD alarm clock or use your MP3 player with an alarm clock and set it for a nice calming song to go off at your child's average wake-up time (as long as it's not before 6:00 a.m.). Let your child choose the song, or consider the "Good Morning!" song on my CD, *The Sweetest Dreams*; it was written just for this purpose. Six o'clock in the morning is the earliest and 7:30 a.m. should be the latest the music goes off. **Don't set it for 7:30 a.m. if your child tends to wake at 6:00 a.m. or earlier.** Explain to your child that having this clock in her room is very special and grown-up ands he's not to touch it. Set it to go off in two minutes to show him what to expect. Put a positive spin on it. Explain that the clock will tell him when it's okay to get out of bed and start the day. Bonus for you: Your child will no longer spend mornings asking, "Is it time to get up yet? Is it time to get up yet?" If you set it for 6:00 a.m. and your child starts to sleep through it, then set the time later and enjoy the extra sleep time yourself!

If you don't like the idea of the music you can purchase an appliance timer (digital ones are presumed to be more accurate) and attach it to a light in your child's room. Explain to her that the light will turn on when it's time to get up. I have successfully used this strategy with children 18 months to 2½ years since the music is often too difficult for this age group to comprehend.

Stickers and Sleep Charts

Kids this age love stickers, stamps, and stars, and tend to respond really well to getting them as a reward for accomplishment. Young kids are happy to receive a star or sticker to press onto a piece of paper or to wear on their clothes, so they can show it off all day. As an extra incentive, you can let your child choose her own reward stickers.

An older child will usually go for a more complex reward system: a chart with squares for each night of a week, for example, that she can decorate and that shows off her track record. Some parents give an assortment of stickers but save the special sparkly gold one as a reward at the end of a good week. To make a weekly chart, turn the paper horizontally, put the days of the week along the top, and the manners down the left, or short, side. (There is a sample chart on page 103 and a blank one you can tear out, copy, and use on page 104.)

Choose four or more "manners" that best apply to your child. I call them manners, rather than rules, because manners connote expected behavior and earning praise. Also, it's a reminder that we want to incorporate manners in our life all the time, not just when we are getting stickers.

You can change the manners over time if you need to, but not so often that you confuse your child about her goals. Use positive terms— *do's*, not *don't's*. In other words, say "Lie quietly in bed" instead of "Don't make noise in bed." Here are a few examples:

- "Lie quietly in bed." (This means no shouting or yelling; talking or humming quietly is okay.)

- "Put yourself to sleep without Mommy or Daddy lying down with you."

- "Put yourself back to sleep during the night without Mommy or Daddy lying down with you."

- "Stay quietly in bed until the wake-up music comes on."

In the beginning, include one easy-to-achieve goal so that your child is guaranteed at least one star and the positive feedback to go with it—such as "Cooperate at bedtime." This is a competence builder. It helps your child feel he can live up to the new sleep expectations, that it's not too hard for him. Raise the bar as he improves. Tell him he's so very, very good at getting that sticker that he now has a new manner to focus on.

Review her sleep manners every night at bedtime, even if your child doesn't seem interested, and review them again promptly the next morning. Give her lots of hugs and praise along with the stickers; after a particularly successful night, you can even offer her a bonus one to wear on her jacket or back of her hand to show to Grandma, the

SLEEP-TIGHT TIP

On occasion an older child will re-spond better to having a privilege taken away as an incentive for changing a sleep behavior (a favorite video, computer time, morning TV). It's a last resort and should only be used with a child who's re-ally resisting making changes or seems not to care. If you have to go there, continue to offer lots of praise for what your child is doing right.

babysitter, her preschool teacher, or the bank teller. After a not-so-great night, don't say or do any-thing to make her feel like she failed. Just tell her that it's okay, she can try again; gently remind her of the behaviors you are look-ing for and that you know she can do it.

A note about "big" rewards. Some parents like to promise them if a child earns a certain number of stickers. This isn't usu-ally necessary—the stickers, the praise, the hugs, and the sense of accomplishment are plenty. If you do want to give an extra reward, make it small and be realistic. If you promise a trip to Disney World, what are you going to do for a follow-up? You're better off promising a trip to the pizza parlor!

The Sleep Lady® Shuffle for Children in a Bed

I'll be honest: It's not as easy to do the Shuffle with a 3- to 5-year-old in a bed as it is with a 6-month-old in a crib. Even though the Shuf-fle is gentle and gradual, older children still get upset and fight the change. If you've got a little resister on your hands, don't get angry, but don't give up either. Keep reminding him that he can learn to put him-self to sleep in his "big boy" bed without Mommy lying down with him.

Throughout the Shuffle we try to minimize tears, but I can't prom-ise to eliminate them completely. Luckily, by the time our children are preschoolers, most of us find it easier to cope with their crying—especially since they're now able to use words to communicate their wants and worries. To keep the tears in check, give lots of reassurance, lots of love, and lots of praise. In addition to reviewing rules and ex-pectations every night at bedtime, you should also pay your child some sleep compliments during the day.

Nights One through Three

Once bath, stories, songs, and review of his sleep manners are over, **sit in a chair or on the floor next to your child's bed**. Stroke or pat him intermittently if he fusses or cries, but don't do it constantly or he'll form a new negative association and will need you to pat him constantly in order to fall asleep. Likewise, don't let him hold your hand: You should control all physical contact. You can be a little more generous with touch the first night, when the whole system is new to him, but be careful about creating difficult new patterns, starting on the second night.

Your child will almost certainly try to engage you. **Try closing your eyes**, which not only conveys an unambiguous message that it's time to sleep, but also makes it easier for you to resist getting drawn into a conversation or philosophical discussion about the nature of the universe. **Stay there until he falls asleep.**

Some children get quite upset if you won't lie down with them. In desperation their parents might put their head down on the pillow next to their child. Try not to do it, and if you do, please limit it to the first night or you aren't going to make much progress. You won't be teaching him new skills if you're sharing a pillow!

Close your eyes and "sh-sh" him. If he continues to reach for you then you may have to scoot your chair away from the bed a bit so that you have to lean in to touch him.

Remember, in three more nights you won't be sitting next to him and won't be able to touch him constantly. You want to be able to fade out of his sleep picture, not add to his fury with every change.

Each time your child wakes during the night respond to him the same way. If he calls for you from his bed, or gets out of bed and comes to your room, take his hand and walk him back to his bed. Remind him that his wake-up music is not on yet and that he needs to lie quietly in his bed and go back to sleep. Sit quietly in your chair by his bed until he does.

NIGHTS ONE THROUGH THREE REMINDERS

- Wake your child if he's not awake by 7:30 a.m. the morning of the day you'll begin sleep coaching.

- Make sure your child gets a good nap on the day of the first night of the Shuffle.

- Create your nap, bedtime, and nighttime sleep plans on pages 59–62.

- Create your sleep manner chart.

- Keep a sleep log.

- Have your family meeting *before* bedtime.

- Plan an early enough bedtime.

- Your first chair position is by the bed.

- There is no time limit on how long you sit by your child at bedtime while he goes to sleep. Minimize your interaction.

- Remember, you *can* hug your child if he gets really worked up! Just don't lie down with him or cuddle him until he goes to sleep.

- Encourage him to pull up his blankets, find his lovey or pacifier, or have a sip of his water by himself.

- Treat each night awakening the same. If your child calls for you from his bed, or gets out of bed and comes to your room, take his hand and walk him back to his bed. Remind him that his wake-up music is not on yet and that he needs to lie quietly in his bed and go back to sleep. Sit quietly in your chair until he does.

- Don't give up until after 6:00 a.m.! Wait until your child's wake-up music or light comes on and then do a dramatic wake-up: leave the room, count to 10, and then come back in as if nothing happened! And remember, if you allow your child to get out of bed and start his day *before* the wake-up music comes on, then he won't take it seriously. After all, you're not, so why should he?

- Each morning go over your child's sleep manners chart before or during breakfast. Make sure you have his attention (the TV should be off) and give him stickers or stars for where he did a good job. Talk to him about the behaviors you want to see more of.

- Start nap coaching on day two.

Nights Four through Six

Children this age do better when they know what to expect, and they also respond to positive reinforcement. Tell your child what a good job he's been doing and that you're going to move your chair. Remind him that you'll still stay in the room until he falls asleep. **Move the chair to the door**.

You may occasionally "sh, sh" if needed, but stay as quiet as you can. Explain to your child that once the lights are out, there's no more talking.

If he gets really upset and you feel he needs help calming down, then go to his bedside, reassure him, and give him a hug. Remind him that you aren't going to leave him and that you'll stay until he falls asleep. Don't let him fall asleep in your arms or on your lap, and don't lie down with him. Keep telling him what a good job he's doing, and how proud you are of him.

Your child may get out of bed and come to your chair. He may try to bring you back to his bed or crawl into your lap. Give him a big hug and tell him that if he'll get back into his bed by himself, you'll come over and tuck him in. If he does it a second or third time, tell him this will be the last time you'll tuck him in.

By this point, most kids get tired and stay in bed, especially if they're getting the message that Mom or Dad is going to stick around until they fall asleep. But if your child *doesn't* stop getting out of bed, stand up and explain clearly that if he keeps it up, you will have to leave. Say something like, "If you don't follow your sleep manners and lie quietly in your bed, then I'm going to have to leave your room." If that doesn't work, there are a couple of things you can try:

- Put a gate in the doorway and sit on the other side of it. Let your child know that if he gets into bed and stays there, you'll come in and tuck him in. If he nods off on the floor near the gate, move him when he's in a sound sleep.

- Stand up and tell your child that if he doesn't get into bed and lie quietly you will leave and close the door. Count to three and give him one more chance to get back in bed. If he doesn't, leave the room, close the door, and stand on the other side of the door and count to 10. Open the door and say calmly, "Get back into your bed and I will come sit in your room." Chances are he'll hop right into bed because he wants you in the room. Some preschoolers will test a parent to see if they'll follow through on the threat, though; if that happens, count to three again, leave the room, close the door, and so on. Some parents have to do this a few times before their child takes them seriously and stays in bed.

Each time your child wakes during the night, respond to him the same way. If he calls for you from his bed, or gets out of bed and comes to your room, take his hand and walk him back to bed. If he calls from the gate, tell him you will come tuck him in if he gets back into bed on his own. Remind him that his wake-up music or light is not on yet and that he needs to lie quietly in his bed and go back to sleep. Sit quietly in your chair by the door until he does.

NIGHTS FOUR THROUGH SIX REMINDERS

- Your chair position is **in the room by the door**.

- Review your child's sleep manners chart at bedtime.

- Keep a sleep log.

- It is common to see a regression the first night you move your chair farther away.

- There are still night awakenings, but you will nonetheless have to move your chair to the door on the fourth night.

- You may get out of your chair and go to your child's bedside to comfort him if he becomes hysterical. Don't stay too long and create a new crutch, such as patting him back to sleep. It happens easily!

- Be careful about your child's efforts to get you to come to his bedside—such as kicking off his blankets and asking you to cover him back up. Put a limit on the number of times you'll comply: "Only two cover ups, honey." Encourage your child to pull up his own blankets, find his lovey or pacifier, or have a sip of his water (put it in a cup where he can reach it) by himself.

- Treat each night awakening the same. If your child calls for you from her bed, or gets out of bed and comes to your room, take her hand and walk her back to her room. Remind her that her wake-up music or light is not on yet and that she needs to lie quietly in bed and go back to sleep. Sit in your chair by the door until she's back asleep.

- Don't give up until after 6:00 a.m.! Wait until the wake-up music comes on and then do a "dramatic wake-up:" Leave the room, count to 10, and come back in as if nothing happened!

- Each morning, review your child's sleep manners chart before or during breakfast. Make sure you have his attention, and give him stickers or stars where he did a good job. Focus on the behavior you want to see more of.

Nights Seven through Nine

Tell your child that he's doing a great job and explain that you're going to move the chair again. Show him where it will be—**in the hallway where he can see it from his bed**. Continue the same soothing techniques, intervening as little as possible. He may cry a bit, but gently reassure him and he will fall asleep. If he keeps getting out of bed and coming to you, tell him you will come tuck him in but he must first get back in bed by himself. If he lies down on the floor, ignore it. Move him to his bed if he falls asleep.

If he continues to get out of bed and come to you in the hallway, consider installing a gate (if you haven't already). Explain to your child that the gate is there to help him remember his sleep manners and to help him stay quietly in his bed. Add that once he remembers all his sleep manners for a whole week (at least) you will take the gate down. Make sure you also explain to him that he may not climb the gate since that is very dangerous. (You'll be sitting right by the gate so you'll also be able to catch any climbing attempts.)

If you do put up a gate, sit on the other side of it at bedtime and for all night awakenings. Don't climb over the gate to hug or reassure your child, until he gets back in bed himself. If you haven't gated your child's door and he comes into your room, take his hand and walk him back to his own room. Remind him that his wake-up music or light is not on yet and he needs to lie quietly in bed and go back to sleep. Tuck him in and sit in your chair in the hall until he's asleep.

NIGHTS SEVEN THROUGH NINE REMINDERS

- Move your chair to the **hallway** *where your child can see you from his bed*.

- Use your voice to reassure him.

- Review your child's sleep manners chart at bedtime.

- Keep a sleep log.

- The move to the hallway can be difficult because you're no longer in the room. Your child may try every trick he can think of to get you back in, including crying, throwing things, or kicking off the blankets and begging to be tucked back in. Set a limit such as "Mommy will only tuck you in one more time and then you will have to do it yourself." Follow through on whatever you say.

- Treat each night awakening the same. If you haven't gated your child's door and he calls for you from his bed or comes into your room, take his hand and walk him back to his own room. Remind him that his wake-up music is not on yet and he needs to lie quietly in bed and go back to sleep. Tuck him in and sit in your chair in the hall until he's asleep.

- If he calls out during the night and there's a gate in his doorway, go to the gate, point out that his wake-up music or light isn't on, and tell him that you'll come into his room and tuck him in if he gets into bed by himself and stays there. If he conks out on the floor near the gate, move him later, when he's sound asleep.

- Don't give up until after 6:00 a.m.! Wait until the wake-up music comes on and then do a dramatic wake-up. If you're already sitting in the hall from an early rising, acknowledge that the wake-up music has now come on and it's time to get up. Remember, if you allow your child to get out of bed before his wake-up music comes on, he won't take the music seriously.

- Each morning, review your child's sleep manners chart with him before or during breakfast. Make sure you have his attention, and give him stickers or stars where he did a good job. Focus on the behavior you want to see more of.

Nights Ten through Twelve

Move a few feet farther down the hallway, so that you're **out of sight but within hearing distance.** Make "sh-sh" sounds from the hallway, just frequently enough that your child knows you're near. If he gets up to look for you, take him back to bed. If you haven't already, put a gate in his doorway if he does it excessively.

Take this step slowly if it really upsets your child. For instance, you can sit halfway out of view and then move completely out of view one or two nights later.

If your child calls for you from his bed or gets out of bed during the night (if you haven't gated his door) and comes to your room, take his hand and walk him back to his room. Point out that his wake-up music or light isn't on yet and remind him that he needs to go back to sleep. Tuck him in and sit quietly in your chair in the hall until he's back asleep. If your child's sleep has improved sufficiently by now (he's waking up less often and for shorter periods) and his room is close enough to yours, you can also try going back to your bed right away and reassuring him from there. If he calls out during the night and you *have* installed a gate, go to the gate, remind him that his wake-up music or light is not on yet and tell him you'll come and tuck him in *if he* gets back in bed and stays there. If he falls asleep on the floor near the gate, move him later when he's sound asleep.

NIGHTS TEN THROUGH TWELVE REMINDERS

- Your chair position on night 10 is in the **hallway** *out of view.*

- Use your voice to reassure your child if needed. Be careful not to shush, talk, or sing constantly until your child is asleep.

- Review your child's sleep manners chart at bedtime.

- Keep a sleep log.

- If your child comes to his doorway to check and see that you're in the hall as promised, but then gets right back in to bed by himself, ignore it.

- Treat each night awakening the same. If your child calls from his bed during the night, or gets out of bed and comes to your room, take his hand and walk him back to his room. Point out that his wake-up music isn't on yet and remind him that he needs to go back to sleep. Tuck him in and sit quietly in your chair in the hall (or go back to your own bed if your room is close enough and reassure him from there).

- If he calls out during the night and you *have* installed a gate, go to the gate, remind him that his wake-up music or light is not on yet, and tell him you'll come in and tuck him in *if he* gets back in bed and stays there. If he falls asleep on the floor near the gate, move him *after* he's sound asleep.

- Don't give up until after 6:00 a.m.!!! Wait until your child's wake-up music comes on and then do dramatic wake-up. If you are already sitting in the hall from an earlier rising, acknowledge that the wake-up music has now come on and that it's time to start the day. Remember, if you allow your child to get out of bed before the music comes on, he won't take it seriously.

- Each morning, review your child's sleep manners chart before or during breakfast. Make sure you have his attention (no TV), give him stickers or stars for his chart, and focus on the behaviors your want to see more of.

- If you've been consistent, by now the night awakenings should be greatly diminished and you may only be struggling with early rising. This is especially true if your child has a previous history of early rising. Early rising can take three to four weeks to improve! Read more about early rising in the "Trouble Shooting" chapter on pages 91–93.

Remember that early rising is caused by one or more of the following:

- a too-late bedtime

- nap deprivation in general

- too much time between the end of the afternoon nap and bedtime (average window is four to five hours for a well-rested child)

- putting your child to bed too drowsy at bedtime

Night Thirteen

A fair number of children start falling asleep and staying asleep between night 10 and 14—occasionally even sooner. But most parents have to take one more step: Put away the chair and leave their child alone for five-minute intervals, or what I call "job checks." To do this, tell your child that you will keep checking on him from his doorway until he's asleep.

Most likely your child won't have a realistic concept of how long five minutes is. It may sound like a very long time, so explain exactly where you'll be during that time and what you'll be doing (brushing your teeth, changing clothes, folding laundry nearby). Always return as promised and check on him from his doorway.

By now your child has had nearly two weeks of preparation. He has given up some of his negative associations and gained quite a bit of sleep independence. He's old enough to understand that you're close by even if you're out of sight. Don't go too far away—stay on the same floor, in a nearby room and just read a magazine or a book for the first few nights. Gradually, you can move a little farther away. If he cries, you'll be back every five minutes to reassure him. Try not to go to the door more than that; he'll just get more stimulated and more upset if he has to say good-bye to you every two minutes.

Unlike the crying-it-out approach to sleep coaching, you don't need to keep stretching out the intervals for longer than five minutes. The only exception is if you sense that five minutes is too brief for your child: that having to see you but separate again every five minutes is making him more agitated. Then experiment and see if he finds it less disturbing if you check on him every 10 or 15 minutes.

Nicholas, age 2 years

CHAPTER TEN

Troubleshooting

We live in a one-bedroom apartment and our baby sleeps in the same room as us. Can we do this while sleep training?

Absolutely! Your chair positions at bedtime can be the same as those outlined in this workbook except for the middle of the night after night four. When your child wakes up during the night after your first three nights by the crib, go to the cribside to do an initial reassuring check and then return to your bed and use your voice to soothe your baby. You could sit up in your bed so he can easily see you.

Some other tricks:

- Put the crib right next to your bed and then move *it* away at the beginning of the Shuffle.

- Use a screen or create a makeshift wall from a curtain tacked to the ceiling.

I need to coach more than one child—and they're in separate bedrooms! Is that possible?

Yes! For example, sleeping coaching a baby and a toddler or pre-schooler at the same time is easier if both parents (or two caregivers) are available at bedtime. Wait for an evening (or ideally a few evenings in a row) when you and your spouse will both be home at bedtime, or recruit a friend or family member to help you. One parent puts the baby to sleep and the other parent puts the toddler/preschooler to sleep using the Shuffle techniques. If you don't have an available and willing spouse or family member to help you, then sleep coach one child at a time. Start with the baby, since he or she goes to bed earlier. Set up your older child with a quiet activity, such as a not-too-stimulating video while you do the Shuffle with the baby at bedtime.

I'm worried that the child I'm sleep coaching will wake my other child. What then?

This is a common concern. Many parents will rush in to soothe one child in order to avoid disturbing the other one. Try not to fall into this trap: It will only perpetuate one child's night awakenings by reinforcing one or both children's sleep crutches. If one child wakes the other, then start with the older child. For instance, if you're working with a 6-month-old and she wakes up a 2-year-old in the process, go to the toddler, reassure him that the baby is okay, and tell him he can go back to sleep—_then_ tend to the 6-month-old. If both parents are home, then divide and conquer, one of you with each child. Don't panic and start any negative habits with your toddler that you'll have to change, such as lying down with him to get him back to sleep quickly and quietly. I also recommend putting a white noise machine in an older child's room to mask the sound of other things going on the house. Marpac makes a good one, or you could use a fan.

My children share a room. How do I sleep train them?

There are several possible scenarios here:

1. If you need to sleep train a baby who's in a crib in your room but will be sharing a room with an older sibling, I suggest you modify the Shuffle and sleep coach your baby in your room and then move her in to the shared room.

2. If your children are already sharing a room, one option is to move the older sibling out temporarily until the baby is consistently sleeping through the night. This option works well if the older sibling already has reasonably good sleep habits. This may mean the older child sleeps in a makeshift bed in your room. Explain to your older child that this arrangement is *temporary*—just until the baby learns how to put himself to sleep. Meanwhile, tell big sister that there will be no talking to or playing with the baby when she moves back into the shared room. Explain that sharing a room is special and it's important to have good "sleep manners."

3. If you're sleep coaching two children at once (singletons or multiples) who share a room (whether they're both in beds or cribs or not), you can still sleep coach at the same time and use the Shuffle techniques. Often one parent will sit between the beds or cribs and go over to the individual bedsides as needed to comfort each child. If both parents are available, you can each sit by one of your child's bedside or crib during the first Shuffle position. You will only need one parent for the subsequent chair positions.

Should I tell my older child that I will be sleep coaching their younger sibling?

Absolutely. Explain to the older child what's going on and help her feel like she's a part of it. Depending on her age and her own sleep skills, you may even help her think of herself as a sleep role model for the baby. Tell her the baby needs to know how to get herself to sleep, just like her big sister does. Explain that when the baby learns, she won't cry as much, but in the meantime you have to be with her, or you have to go check on her. The older child will let you go more easily if you make her an ally.

What if my child gets sick in the middle of sleep training?

Don't abandon the program completely: If you can, maintain your Shuffle position until he feels better. If you feel he absolutely needs you closer, go back to sitting near his crib or bed as you did on the first three nights of the Shuffle and then move to the door when he is feeling better. Don't draw this out or you will just make it harder for him. If he gets sick shortly after you complete his coaching, he'll probably backslide a bit and you may have to do an abbreviated version of the Shuffle to get him sleeping all night again.

When your child is sick, respond immediately to his cries at night. Do whatever you need to do—give him medicine, aspirate his nose, clean him up after a tummy attack. Hold and comfort him as much as you think he needs, even if it sets back sleep training a few days. Soothe and take care of your child but try not to totally regress.

My child consistently wakes up before 6:00 a.m. What's going on?

It's likely your child is getting to bed too late, getting too little sleep during the day, is awake for too long between his afternoon nap and bedtime, or is being put down too asleep at bedtime. Check your sleep log to make sure he's getting enough daytime sleep and going to bed early enough and awake enough to really master the skill of putting himself to sleep. Children 5 years and under should generally be going to bed between 7:00 p.m. and 8:00 p.m.

If your child is older than 6 months and has been getting up and staying up earlier than 6:00 a.m. for several months, you have an established pattern that will probably take three to four weeks to change.

You will have to work on naps and bedtime at the same time as the early-morning awakenings.

What to do:

- Put up room-darkening shades. This alone can make a big difference.

- When your child wakes up, go in initially at (for example) 5:00 a.m. and say, "It's not time to get up." Point out that the wake-up music or light isn't on (if you're using either of them). Depending on your child's age, you might say, "Mommy and Daddy are sleeping."

- If you're in the process of the Shuffle, then after your brief initial check resume your chair position until the wake-up music or light comes on.

- If you believe that staying in your child's room during these early risings is keeping him up then consider leaving. In that case, when he wakes up, go into his room, remind him of his wake-up music, offer him his lovey and verbal and physical reassurance, and then leave the room. Make your visit brief, so as not to further awaken him. Go in for brief checks every 15 to 20 minutes until 6:00 a.m., when you make it your final visit. At that point go into the room and say, "Good morning! Your wake-up music is on." Excitedly open the shades and get your child up to start the day. Don't talk about or refer to your prior visits. I call this a dramatic wake-up. Act as if nothing terribly important has happened. With this routine, you're conveying the following message to your child: Getting you out of bed has nothing to do with how long you have been crying: it is because it's wake-up time.

   If you prefer not to use wake-up music and your child is 3 years or older, you can also get a simple clock and draw a picture of what 6:00 a.m. looks like on a clock face. Set your drawing right next to the clock so it can be seen from the child's bed. Review each night at bedtime that he is to stay in bed until 6:00 a.m.

   I find using a clock radio/CD player or a light with a timer is more concrete and easier for a child to understand. Remind him that he must stay in bed until the music or light comes on. Some parents have used the light successfully with 2-year-olds.

Couldn't I fix the early-rising problem by simply putting my child to bed later?

Unfortunately, no! The only time that might work is if the following apply:

- Your child is taking "good naps" (determined by age).

- Your child appears rested and happy during the day with less than the average night's sleep for the child's age group.

- Your child consistently sleeps through the night and is not off the sleep average by more than one hour.

- You child seems rested and ready to start his day at 6:00 a.m. and can make it to nap time without getting too sleepy.

My child soaks through his diapers at night. What should I do?

Try using extra-absorbent overnight diapers or a larger-size diaper with an insert, or "doubler,"—a pad that you can stick in the diaper. They can be handy on long car or plane trips as well. If you *have* to change your child's diaper and you're fast at it, you might be able to remove a soaked diaper quickly while your baby is sound asleep without taking him out of his crib or bed. If your child is over 2, talk to your pediatrician to rule out sleep apnea, which can increase bedwetting.

My child poops every time I put him in his crib. What should I do?

Some children dirty their diaper just as you put them to bed at night or nap time—and some parents become convinced it's intentional, that the child knows you will pick him up and get him out of the crib. Obviously you need to change the diaper, but do it as quietly as you can, in light as dim as possible. If you can manage it, change him in the bed or crib, and then hand him his lovey and return to your Shuffle position. If this happens at nap time, change him, but approach it as a too-short nap and follow the nap-training advice in the "Nap Coaching" chapter. If it happens at 5:00 a.m., change him and follow the advice for early risers. Children often have a hard time going back to sleep after a 30-minute nap and then a diaper change, or after a 5:00 a.m. diaper change. You may see some crying, but stay consistent and reassuring. If you have completed the Shuffle and you feel your child needs a little more reassurance than normal to go back to sleep after his diaper change, then it's okay to sit closer that night if you feel it will help. On the following night return to your usual routine.

My child vomits when I put her into her crib. What should I do?

A lot of parents worry that if they let their babies cry too long, they will vomit, particularly if the child has or had reflux. This may be the case if you leave a child to cry on her own, but it seldom happens when the parent remains in the room and practices my gentler, more gradual method. To alleviate this problem, don't feed your baby right before sleep.

Some children, even older babies, vomit on purpose because they know the parent will take them out of their crib and fuss over them. If you see your child trying to make herself gag (some kids can do this without using fingers!), firmly say, "No!" but immediately follow up with soothing reassurance. If she does throw up, keep cleanup as quick as possible, and engage with her as little as possible. Use wipes or a washcloth, if you can, rather than getting her completely up for a bath. Don't turn the lights on. Some parents leave an extra sheet on the floor for children who tend to vomit over the crib railing. This makes cleanup easier since they can just roll it up and toss it in the hamper. Then reassure your child back to sleep. Remember, you don't want to give the message that if she throws up she will get out of the crib and not have to go to sleep.

Obviously, this doesn't apply to a child who is sick. In that case, you need to comfort her and follow your doctor's timetable for giving her fluids.

I have a very alert, very bright baby. How will this effect sleep training?

Occasionally, unusually alert, bright, and aware children have trouble learning to sleep. These are the children who reach their physical milestones on the early side, and they tend to have more fragmented sleep. Temperamentally, they may be the kind of children who know what they want and when they want it, and are willing to hold out until they get it. If this sounds like your child, make sure you don't fall into the trap of thinking that she needs less sleep than average. She may have a hard time shutting out the world in order to get to sleep. Room-darkening shades and a sound screen can help for naps. Be extremely vigilant about watching for your baby's sleep window.

My child can't seem to settle down at all when I sit by his crib. What do I do?

If you're absolutely convinced after a few days of sitting in your child's room that your presence is overstimulating to him, *or* you find it so hard to do it yourself that you can't be consistent, then I suggest you either have the other parent try, or you leave the room and do timed checks on your child. There is no magic rule about how often you check or how many times you check, and you may have to experiment a bit. If you check on him too soon, he may treat it like a game and get even more stimulated. If you are away too long, he may get himself quite worked up and upset. I suggest that you start with every seven minutes and gradually increase it, but trust your own instincts and make necessary adjustments; this isn't a one-size-fits-all approach. When you check on him, go right into the room to his crib. Give him a quick reassuring pat, but don't linger. You will defeat the whole purpose if you stand there for a half hour patting him to sleep.

Here's another variant: Sometimes the Shuffle works at night but not for naps. The child is more awake, and more likely to keep trying to engage. So feel free to stick to the Shuffle at night, and use the timed checks I just described for the naps if that's what feels right to you.

Safe-Sleeping Recommendations for Babies

Here are some tips for baby sleep safety. Most of this information is from the American Academy of Pediatrics and First Candle. I'd like to emphasize that this advice is primarily for healthy infants. Always talk to your doctor, particularly if your child was premature or has any health problems or unique circumstances. Recommendations have changed over the years as we have learned more about child safety and development, and they may well change again, so revisit safety issues with your doctor frequently. You may see all kinds of contradictory information on parenting and health websites. A good place to sort it all out is the American Academy of Pediatrics parenting corner: http://www.aap.org/parents.html.

1. Back to sleep. Always place your baby on his back to sleep—both at naps and at night. Side and tummy positions are not safe. This is absolutely essential to reduce the risk of sudden infant death syndrome (SIDS). Once your baby rolls over consistently backward and forward you won't be able to keep him on his back all the time, unless that's his preferred sleeping position, so make sure he has enough room to move around and there are no unsafe items in his crib. Unsafe items include quilts, loose blankets, soft bedding, pillows, soft or pillowlike bumpers, and stuffed animals or toys with pieces that can come off.

2. Babies should sleep on a firm surface, such as a safety-approved crib mattress, covered by a tight-fitting crib sheet. Never place your baby to sleep on pillows, quilts, sheepskins, or other soft surfaces. Infants should never sleep or nap on adult beds, waterbeds, sofas, or soft mattresses.

3. Be careful about buying or using secondhand cribs, bassinets, or co-sleepers, even if they've been in the family for years. Safety standards have changed and some products have been recalled or taken off the market. Contact the Consumer Product Safety Commission at 1-800-638-2772 or at http:// www.cpsc.gov http://www.cpsc.gov. *Consumer Reports* has also reminded parents that co-sleepers have not been tested as of this writing.

4. You'll see numerous devices and gadgets on the market that claim to help a baby maintain a safe sleep position, but they have not all been tested for safety and efficacy, and are not recommended. Generally, avoid them. If you have some specific concern about your child's sleep position or movement, talk to your doctor.

5. Cribs should be placed in a warm, dark part of the room, away from windows. Blankets should not dangle from the side of the crib, and wall hangings need to be well out of a baby's reach so she can't pull them down on herself. Keep soft objects, toys, and loose bedding out of your baby's sleep area. Don't use pillows, blankets, quilts, sheepskins, or pillowlike crib bumpers (other than the small blanket you swaddle a newborn in, and that should be away from the face). They all pose a risk of suffocation.

6. At 6 months, remove all crib mobiles or toys attached to crib sides because once the baby can pull and grab, they become a hazard. In fact, I like keeping mobiles away from the crib all the time; use them someplace where she's awake. Make the crib or sleep area "boring" as well as safe.

7. Do not let your baby overheat during sleep. Keep room temperatures at what would be comfortable for a lightly clothed adult. Once you stop swaddling your baby, use a microfleece

sleep sack or blanket sleeper. If the bedroom is cooler, use two sleep sacks or place one over the pajamas or onesies.

8. Remember that the American Academy of Pediatrics, strongly recommends that you do not smoke around your baby and should not allow anyone else to smoke around your baby. Smoking exposure may increase the risk of SIDS and other respiratory illnesses.

9. The American Academy of Pediatrics recommends that babies *not* sleep in a bed or on a couch or armchair with adults or other children. But it's fine to have an infant close by in your room, particularly in the early months. (See my advice on room sharing in *Good Night, Sleep Tight* for more information.) If you bring your baby into bed with you to breastfeed, put him back in a separate sleep area, such as a bassinet, crib, cradle, or a bedside co-sleeper (infant bed that attaches to an adult bed) when finished. When he starts to roll and move in his sleep, graduate to a standard crib for better—and safer—sleeping.

Remember that beds that are perfectly safe and comfortable for adults or older children can be very hazardous for babies. Soft bedding and other items in the adult bed increase the risk of SIDS and suffocation, especially for young babies. A baby or small child can also fall from the bed or get trapped between the mattress and the structure of the bed (the headboard, footboard, side rails, and frame), between the bed and the wall or nearby furniture, or even between railings in the headboard or footboard. Fatalities have been documented.

If you do choose to have your baby in the family bed, understand all the bed-sharing safety rules and *always follow them*. Parents who do have a baby in bed with them for even part of the night must never smoke or use substances, such as alcohol or drugs (including prescription drugs that make you sleep heavily), that may impair arousal, making them less aware of their baby's needs or position in the bed.

10. Pacifiers can significantly reduce the risk of SIDS (see www.firstcandle.org). They also soothe infants. Talk to your pediatrician about when to start—and stop—the pacifier. Many doctors advise using a clean pacifier when putting the infant down to sleep, although you shouldn't force the baby to take it. If you're breastfeeding, wait four to six weeks before introducing a pacifier. Many parents stop the pacifier after 6 months, so the baby doesn't get so accustomed to falling asleep with something in his mouth. (Medical advice has changed frequently over the years, so make sure you raise this topic with your doctor and check back as the child gets older.)

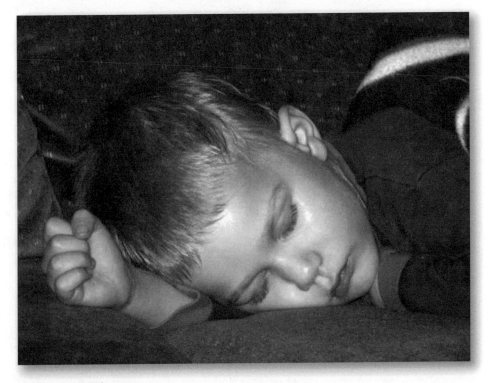

Kaden, age 3½ years

CHAPTER ELEVEN

Sleep Logs, Sleep Manner Chart, and Certificate of Completion

Emmalee, age 3½ years

Sleep Log

ACTIVITY (meal, nap, bed)	WHAT HAPPENED	AWAKE/ START	ASLEEP TIME	TOTAL TIME
Bedtime	Nursed well; cried on and off; picked up once	7:00 p.m.	7:30 p.m.	
Woke	Nursed well; cried on and off; picked up once	3:00 a.m.	3:40 a.m.	
Woke	Whimpered	5:40 a.m.	Dramatic wake-up at 6:00 a.m.	

Sleep Log

ACTIVITY (meal, nap, bed)	WHAT HAPPENED	AWAKE/ START	ASLEEP TIME	TOTAL TIME

Max's Sleep Manners

	Monday	Tuesday	Wednesday	Thursday	Friday	Saturday	Sunday
Cooperates at bedtime							
Lies quietly in bed							
Puts self to sleep without Mommy or Daddy lying down with him							
Puts self back to sleep during the night							
Stays in bed quietly until the wake-up music comes on							

Sleep Manners _____

	Monday	Tuesday	Wednesday	Thursday	Friday	Saturday	Sunday

The Good Night, Sleep Tight
Award of Achievement is Presented to

for

An Outstanding Night's Sleep!

The Sleep Lady®
Kim West, LCSW-C

CHAPTER TWELVE

Resources

Books

GENERAL BABY AND CHILD CARE

American Academy of Pediatrics. *Caring for Your Baby and Young Child: Birth to Age 5*, 4th ed. Bantam Books, 2005.

Schmitt, Barton D., MD. *Your Child's Health: The Parent's One-Stop Reference Guide to Symptoms, Emergencies, Common Illnesses, Behavior Problems, and Healthy Development.* 2nd ed. Bantam, 2005.

BEDTIME

Bauer, Marion Dane. *Sleep, Little One, Sleep.* Simon and Schuster, 2002.

Bentley, Dawn. *Good Night, Sweet Butterflies.* Simon and Schuster, 2003.

Boynton, Sandra. *Snoozers: 7 Short Short Stories for Lively Little Kids.* Little Simon, 1997.

Brown, Margaret Wise. *A Child's Good Night Book.* HarperCollins, 2000.

———. *Goodnight Moon.* HarperFestival, 1991.

Dillard, Sarah (illustrator). *Ten Wishing Stars: A Countdown to Bedtime Book.* Intervisual Press, 2003.

Good Night, Baby!, Soft-to-Touch Books, DK Publishing, 1995.

Fox, Mem. *Time for Bed.* Red Wagon Books, 1997.

Hague, Kathleen. *Good Night, Fairies.* Seastar Books, 2002.

Inkpen, Mick. *It's Bedtime, Wibbly Pig.* Viking, 2004.

Lewis, Kim. *Good Night, Harry.* Candlewick Press, 2004.

McBratney, Sam. *Guess How Much I Love You.* Candlewick Press, 1996.

McCue, Lisa. *Snuggle Bunnies.* Reader's Digest, 2003.

McMullen, Nigel. *It's Too Soon!* Simon and Schuster, 2004.

Meyer, Mercer. *Just Go to Bed.* Golden Books, 2001.

Munsch, Robert. *Love You Forever.* Firefly Books, 1986.

Paul, Ann Whitford. *Little Monkey Says Good Night.* Farrar, Straus and Giroux, 2003.

Penn, Audrey. *The Kissing Hand.* Child and Family Press, 2006.

Rathmann, Peggy. *Good Night, Gorilla.* G. P. Putnam's Sons, 2000.

———. *10 Minutes Till Bedtime.* G. P. Putnam's Sons, 2001.

Steinbrenner, Jessica. *My Sleepy Room.* Handprint Books, 2004.

Trapani, Iza. *Twinkle, Twinkle, Little Star.* Charlesbridge Publishing, 1998.

BREASTFEEDING

American Academy of Pediatrics, Joan Younger Meek, MD, and Sherill Tippins. *The American Academy of Pediatrics New Mother's Guide to Breastfeeding.* Bantam, 2005.

Gromada, Karen Kerkhoff. *Mothering Multiples: Breastfeeding and Caring for Twins or More!,* 3rd ed. La Leche League International Book, 2007.

Huggins, Kathleen. *The Nursing Mother's Companion,* rev. ed. Harvard Common Press, 2005.

La Leche League International. *Womanly Art of Breastfeeding,* 7th ed. LLLI, 2004.

Mohrbacher, Nancy, and Kathleen Kendall-Tackett. *Breastfeeding Made Simple: Seven Natural Laws for Nursing Mothers.* New Harbinger Publications, 2005.

Newman, Jack, MD, and Teresa Pitman. *The Ultimate Breastfeeding Book of Answers: The Most Comprehensive Problem-Solving Guide to Breastfeeding from the Foremost Expert in North America,* rev. ed. Three Rivers Press, 2006.

Pryor, Gale, and Kathleen Huggins. *Nursing Mother, Working Mother,* rev. ed. Harvard Common Press, 2007.

West, Diana, and Lisa Marasco. *The Breastfeeding Mother's Guide to Making More Milk.* Foreword by Martha Sears, RN. McGraw-Hill, 2008.

NEW SIBLING

Ballard, Robin. *I Used to Be the Baby.* Greenwillow, 2002.

Bourgeois, Paulette, and Brenda Clark. *Franklin's Baby Sister.* Scholastic, 2000.

Brown, Marc. *Arthur's Baby.* Little, Brown, 1990.

Henkes, Kevin. *Julius, the Baby of the World.* HarperTrophy, 1995.

London, Jonathan. *Froggy's Baby Sister.* Viking, 2003.

Meyer, Mercer. *The New Baby.* Golden Books, 2001.

MUSIC FOR RELAXATION AND BEDTIME ROUTINE

Ackerman, William. *The Opening of Doors.* Windham Hill Records, 1992.

Baby's First Lullabies. Twin Sisters, 2005.

Disney Baby Lullaby: Favorite Sleepytime Songs for Baby and You. Walt Disney Records, 1992.

Falkner, Jason. *Bedtime with the Beatles: Instrumental Versions of Classic Beatles Songs.* Sony Wonder, 2001.

Golden Slumbers: A Father's Lullaby. Rendezvous, 2002.

Malia, Tina. *Lullaby Favorites: Music for Little People.* Music for Little People, 1997.

Music for Babies—Sleepy Baby. Big Kids Productions, 2002.

Parents: The Lullaby Album. Angel Records, 1993.

Solnik, Tanja. *From Generation to Generation: A Legacy of Lullabies in Yiddish, Ladino, and Hebrew*. Dreamsong Recordings, 1993; *Lullabies and Love Songs*. Dreamsong Recordings, 1996.

Stroman, Paige. *Lullabies to Celebrate Mother and Child.* National Music Marketing/Lullabyland, 2001.

West, Kim, John Judge and Jim Conley. *The Sweetest Dreams.*, Sleep Lady Solutions LLC, 2008.

Websites

American Academy of Pediatrics
www.AAP.org
The official site with advice and information about a multitude of pediatric topics. Resources, books, and videos are available on this site.

American Academy of Sleep Medicine (formerly the American Sleep Disorders Association)
www.aasmnet.org
The website of this membership group of doctors and other professionals contains links to sleep resources and research and also directs patients to accredited sleep disorder centers (not all of which treat children). Click "Patients and Public" to see a list of sleep disorder clinics.

Consumer Product Safety Commission

www.cpsc.gov

List of product recalls and safety requirements for various products such as cribs.

First Candle Organization: Helping Babies Survive and Thrive

www.firstcandle.org 800-221-7437

National Sleep Foundation

www.sleepfoundation.org

This nonprofit group addresses numerous sleep issues for children and adults. The website includes the group's new childhood sleep guidelines.

Information on Postpartum Depression

Medical Education on Postpartum Depression

www.MedEdPPD.org

An education website developed with the support of the National Institute of Mental Health. Updated information and resources for care providers and women with postpartum depression.

Postpartum Support International

www.postpartum.net

Nationwide Helpline: 1-800-944-4PPD (4773)

Provides current information, resources, and education. Volunteer coordinators in every U.S. state and 26 countries that offer local support groups.

The Good Night, Sleep Tight

Award of Achievement is Presented to

for

An Outstanding Night's Sleep!

The Sleep Lady®
Kim West, LCSW-C